Surrounded by Reality
The Best of Doug Moe on Madison

Surrounded by Reality

The Best of Doug Moe on Madison

**J O N E S
B O O K S**

Madison, Wisconsin

Jones Books
309 N. Hillside Terrace
Madison, Wisconsin 53705
www.jonesbooks.com

Book design by Janet Trembley

First edition, first printing

Library of Congress Cataloging-in-Publication Data

Moe, Doug.
    Surrounded by reality : the best of Doug Moe on Madison / Doug Moe.
        p. cm.
    Summary: 80 columns written by Doug Moe for the Capital times in
Madison, Wisconsin.
    ISBN 0-9763539-3-8 (alk. paper)
    I. Title.
    PN4874.M575A25 2005
    814'.6—dc22
                                                                2005024308

Printed in the United States of America

Table of Contents

2001

2002

2003

2004

2005

Surrounded by Reality

Introduction

The job of newspaper columnist first cast its spell on me in a booth in the Kollege Klub late in my career at UW–Madison.

Not many people knew the KK was open for breakfast, and I would sit in solitude with my coffee and a copy of the *Chicago Sun-Times,* purchased a half block away at Rennebohm's.

This was the late 1970s. I was getting dangerously close to graduating, and still didn't know what I wanted to do out in the real world.

I enjoyed losing myself in the wonderful tales told by the *Sun-Times'* lead columnists, the great Mike Royko and his colleague Roger Simon.

Simon had wonderful leads. I recall him doing a column on how one of the Watergate burglars was getting rich giving speeches. "Some countries put their criminals in prison," Simon wrote. "We put ours on speaking tours." When Geraldo Rivera went into Al Capone's vault for a televised special, Simon began his next day's column: "I knew we were in trouble when he called an old whiskey bottle an artifact."

Royko was known for his tough columns on politicians, but I loved the columns he devoted to ordinary people caught in extraordinary, and often funny, circumstances. One was about a Chicago computer operator who, walking one morning to catch his train to work, found himself blocked by a long, slow-moving freight train. The man decided to climb on the freight and jump off on the other side, but once he was on the train it began to pick up speed, and the man ended up in Iowa with his sack lunch and $1.45 in his pocket. Another favorite was the woman who kept getting court notices to bring her child into court to confront accusations of child neglect. The problem was the woman did not have any children. Royko advised her that the court would never believe that. Better to rent a monkey, put the monkey in baby clothes, and take it to court. The judge might feel sorry for her. "And who knows," Royko wrote. "Someday you might be proud. The kid could grow up to be an alderman."

I read those columns and many more, and one day the light clicked on: That's what I wanted to do.

Of course, nobody gets to start out as a columnist. After graduating, I spent 15-plus years in the magazine business, first as a full-time freelancer, then as associate editor, and finally editor of *Madison* magazine.

I enjoyed writing for magazines, but the journalists I looked up to were still the newspaper columnists. I expanded my horizons past Chicago, reading columns and collections by writers like Jimmy Breslin, Pete Hamill, Damon Runyon, Herb Caen, Red Smith, and Jim Murray. The *Sun-Times* picked up a couple of other guys I really liked, Tom Fitzpatrick and John Schulian. I also read about columnists, in books like Neil Grauer's *Wits and Sages* and Karl E. Meyer's Pundits, *Poets & Wits*.

In 1996, my magazine was sold, and though I got along with the new owners, it seemed like a good time to take Dave Zweifel, the editor of the *Capital Times*, up on a long-standing lunch invitation.

It didn't happen immediately, but the end result of

that lunch was my writing a daily column on page two of the *Capital Times*. If people haven't seen it, they'll ask what the column is about. The simple answer is Madison—the city's people, issues, history, and quirks. But that hardly says it all. Writing about Madison gives me a surprisingly broad range. In this book you'll find a column about the man who got rich writing the Oscar Mayer wiener jingle as well as one about a young hitchhiker who'd decided to try to start her life over in Madison, but never made it to the city. Taken together, I hope these columns offer a fair view of recent and not-so-recent life in Madison—the best place to live on the planet, in my admittedly biased opinion.

The column began in May 1997 as an "items" column—thank you, Herb Caen—short, brisk anecdotes separated by three dots. More than eight years and 2,500 columns later, I still do occasional "items" columns, but more often than not, the column is now devoted to a single subject. It's the best of those columns that make up this book.

Still, when you write six a week, you have to use all the tools at your disposal. I'm often asked about that. How do you write so many? I guess the answer is that if I thought about doing six a week, or 25 a month, or 300 a year, I might not be able to do it. My attitude is I have to write one today, and I don't think beyond that.

People also want to know if I have some columns stored in advance, just in case. The answer is no. A column written a month ago inevitably reads like it. Breslin has pointed out that writing on deadline gives energy to your prose, even if the subject happens to be historical.

I'd like to thank Dave Zweifel for taking me to lunch a decade ago, and also for making the *Capital Times* feel almost instantly like home. Thanks as well to managing editor Phil Haslanger and to the city desk editors—especially Ron McCrea, Chris Murphy, and Joe Hart—who have handled the columns over the years, kindly laughing in the right places and spotting various stupidities before they made their way into print. It's a cliché to thank your readers, but it's one I can't resist. Thanks for the tips, the feedback, the friendship.

For their help in making this book a reality, my thanks to Joan Strasbaugh of Jones Books, who has brought her abundant energy and matchless book business savvy to two of my projects now; and to my friend Mark Schmitz, one of the country's best graphic designers, for his inspired work on the cover.

The columns appear in chronological order with the exception of the first and last, which deal with Madison's square mileage and its enduring reputation of being "surrounded by reality." Sounds like a good book title to me.

One last note: A month before I wrote my first newspaper column, Mike Royko died. Eventually I got to write and publish a book about him, and who wrote a highly favorable review of that book in the *Chicago Tribune?* Royko's old colleague Roger Simon. Don't tell me dreams can't come true.

═══════════

Thursday, December 16, 1999

How Many Miles Surrounded by Reality?

I was scanning a press release earlier this week about a Madison native in the entertainment business. At one point the release said Madison was "once described as 15 square miles surrounded by reality."

The Best of Doug Moe on Madison

This has haunted us for more than 20 years, and with the end of the world as we know it only two weeks away, it may be the last chance to set the record straight.

Lee Dreyfus gets the original blame. "It was during the campaign," Bill Kraus was saying Wednesday. Kraus rode shotgun for Dreyfus both during his 1978 run for governor and after the UW–Stevens Point chancellor was elected. Dreyfus has long since left Madison, but Kraus stayed.

"I don't remember the precise context," Kraus said. "But somebody brought up Madison and Dreyfus said it was 30 square miles surrounded by reality."

Dreyfus himself was not famous as a realist. He got elected in the first place because Kraus and Bob Williams and a few other savvy politicos who liked to get out of Stevens Point once in a while thought Bob Kasten was vulnerable in the Republican primary. He sure was vulnerable. Kasten was having his yard signs made for the general election on the day Dreyfus stomped him in the primary.

When Dreyfus decamped after one term, the rest of us were stuck with his glib remark. That's bad enough, but whenever it's brought up, which is often, people get it wrong. Not to mention that Dreyfus had it wrong in the first place.

In a 1995 guest column in the *Capital Times*, County Executive Rick Phelps wrote, "When Governor Dreyfus characterized Madison as 78 square miles surrounded by reality . . ."

Bill Geist was head of the convention bureau in 1991 when he told a reporter, "Madison really is 50 square miles surrounded by reality and that's how we try to market it."

Radio personality John "Sly" Sylvester, asked in 1995 what he had learned after a decade on the air, said, "Madison is 25 square miles surrounded by reality."

Gene Parks, in a 1998 letter to this paper, noted that people sometimes say Madison is "24 square miles surrounded by reality."

Gary Knowles, then with state tourism, noted in 1991 that Madison is "62 square miles surrounded by reality."

Even John Patrick Hunter, a beloved figure in this newsroom who visits often with his wife, Merry, wrote in 1990 that Scott Klug's upset of Bob Kastenmeier meant Dreyfus would "have to revise his put-down" of Madison as "23 square miles surrounded by reality."

When I saw the "15 miles" press release this week, after issuing a primal scream, I called the city Planning and Development Department. Bill Lanier, a geographic information specialist—"I work with maps"—was good enough to help me out.

"As of January 1, 1999, 67.24 square miles," Lanier said. "But do you have a minute?"

Of course. I'm a columnist.

"Then hold on," Lanier said. "Let me punch some stuff up. We have a map of the city in an electronic format, and one of the features is the boundary of the municipality."

After a moment, Lanier said, "There's one thing. It's going to give it in feet."

Bring it on.

Another minute passed. Then Lanier said, "One billion, 917 million, 289 thousand and 645 square feet."

In the 2002 gubernatorial campaign, we can look forward to Scott McCallum dismissing Jim Doyle by saying, "We all know Doyle's from Madison, 1,917,289,645 square feet surrounded by reality."

It works out to 68.78 square miles. Surrounded by reality, of course.

1997

Saturday, December 6, 1997

The Riddle of Otis Redding
The Soul Great Crashed into Lake Monona and Died 30 Years Ago with His Band — But the Legend Lingers

It is the stuff of Madison legend, and it is a legend that has neither faded nor been fully resolved in the three decades since a twin-engine Beechcraft plunged into Lake Monona on December 10, 1967.

That one of the seven people killed in the crash was 26-year-old Otis Redding, one of the world's hottest young soul singers, ensured that the events of that dank, misty day, 30 years ago next Wednesday, would pass into myth.

Stories told, retold, embellished, invented. Did anyone survive? Were drugs found on board? What became of the massive amounts of cash that Redding was known to carry? Was Redding himself at the controls of the plane, as an

Surrounded by Reality

Esquire magazine article once asserted?

Otis Redding was the discovery of promoter Phil Walden. As a teen in the late '50s, Otis was going by the name Rockhouse and playing segregated clubs around his native Macon, Georgia. Walden brought him to Memphis and Stax studio, where Redding recorded his first hit, "These Arms of Mine," in 1962.

By 1967, there was no stopping him. He was huge in Europe and on the U.S. college circuit, and in early December Redding was in the studio in Memphis recording an album containing a soul ballad he was convinced would break him through to white audiences and superstardom. He'd begun writing it while living in a boathouse in San Francisco. He called it "(Sittin' on) the Dock of the Bay."

After finished the song in the studio December 7, Redding began a planned tour with his band, the Bar-Kays. They played a gig in Nashville, and early on the morning of December 9 flew to Cleveland. They played three shows Saturday night and slept in. At 12:30 Sunday afternoon, the singer, six members of the band, and pilot Richard Fraser boarded the twin-engine Beechcraft at Cleveland's Hopkins Field and headed for Madison.

They were to play two shows at The Factory, a West Gorham Street club where Canterbury Booksellers now stands. Their scheduled warm-up band, The Grim Reapers, later gained fame as Cheap Trick.

Sometime after 3 p.m., with the plane 10 miles south of the Madison airport, flight control was transferred from Chicago Federal Aviation Control to Madison. At 3:25, when the plane was four miles south of the Madison airport, above Squaw Bay, the pilot was given clearance to land. That was the plane's last communication.

Three minutes later, Bernard Reese, a resident of the 4600 block of Tonyawatha Trail in Monona, standing in his backyard, heard a sputtering engine in the fog and low clouds above Lake Monona. Suddenly a plane flashed through the

2

overcast sky, its left wing dipping, and hit the water with a loud bang about a half mile off the southeast shore. It rested on the surface for several minutes and then sank, by which time Reese had run inside and phoned the police.

It took the police boat with four officers 17 minutes to reach the site. The officer steering, Charles Campbell, was a pilot himself and familiar with the approach path. They ran into debris and one man floating with the help of a cushion—Bar-Kay trumpeter Ben Cauley, 20, the only survivor.

Cauley's recollections are included in the official Madison police reports of the crash. Sergeant Ted Mell, one of the officers in the boat, noted that along with Cauley, two others were found floating, not breathing, in the water—Bar-Kay Jimmie King and the pilot. From Mell's report: "They located no other survivors; however, they did pick up a small dark gray attaché case."

Redding's wife, Zelma, flew to Madison the next day with Twiggs Lyndon, who worked for Phil Walden, Otis's manager. After visiting Cauley in his Methodist Hospital room, the two went to the morgue—Otis's body had been found. He was strapped into the cockpit next to the pilot's seat and had not been flying the plane himself, as *Esquire* writer Robert Sam Anson had speculated.

From the report of officer Ralin Phillips: "There was a head wound on Redding, right between his eyes, plus several other cuts around his face and neck. The right leg was also broken. A search of the body of Redding produced one Bulova watch, one black leather billfold, and $302 in cash." Also what appeared to be a package of marijuana, Phillips noted.

Zelma Redding wanted to know about the large amounts of cash Otis would have been carrying from the Nashville and Cleveland shows. A December 13, 1967, article in the *Capital Times* contained this passage: "Still missing is Redding's attaché case . . . which his wife, Zelma, and

3

booking agent, Twiggs Lyndon, said he carried on the plane."

Was that the "small dark gray attaché case" referred to in Sergeant Mell's earliest report of the crash? I put that question to Mell in 1983, and he responded, "To be frank with you, I don't even remember any attaché case." At the time I also asked a Monona officer who worked the case, William Diebold, the same question. "You want something for the record on that attaché case?" he said. "You won't get it."

On December 13, a federal aviation investigator complained to Phillips that someone had rifled through luggage recovered from the crash. From Phillips's later report: "I later checked at the station and was informed that officers had been dispatched . . . to search this luggage for the money Mrs. Redding had reported her deceased husband had been carrying."

Yet there is no police report on such a search.

In the end, no great sums of cash were found—or if they were, they stayed with those who found them. All the bodies were eventually recovered. The police reports referred to marijuana on the plane, but a 1981 article in the *Madison Music Guide* said cocaine and opium were found as well. I can find no other mention of them, and no officers involved in the investigation ever spoke on the record about drugs other than marijuana.

The month after the crash, Phil Walden and Twiggs Lyndon released "(Sittin on) the Dock of the Bay" and it was the huge smash Redding had predicted, topping the *Billboard* Hot 100 chart for several weeks running and selling more than a million copies.

But Lyndon, who had come to Madison with Otis' wife, was headed for trouble. He stabbed a man and went to prison, and upon getting out died in a skydiving accident some believed to be suicide. Friends said he feared growing old.

Walden had problems as well. His Capricorn Records

went through bankruptcy, and another of his stars, Duane Allman, died in a motorcycle accident in 1980. Capricorn Records survived, though, and Walden as president recently gave the Associated Press a nice quote about the "magnificence" of Redding's music. A 1992 CD, *The Very Best of Otis Redding,* sold more than 500,000 copies.

A reporter tracked down Ben Cauley, the one survivor of the crash, in 1992. Cauley and his wife, Shirley, were living in Memphis and had seven children. Cauley said he was working as a studio musician.

In 1986, the city of Madison erected some memorial benches in Redding's honor in Law Park. Last summer, with the opening of Monona Terrace, the benches were relocated—and rededicated —in the Evjue Gardens atop the convention center.

Zelma Redding didn't make it back to Madison for either tribute. Now 55, she lives on a 440-acre ranch outside of Macon. She said fans still show up to pay their respects to her husband, the soul legend who died 30 years ago in the frigid waters of Lake Monona. She recently told a reporter that kids who weren't even born when Otis died come and stare at the marble tomb where he rests, a short walk from the ranch.

The visitors weep, and when they've gone, Zelma does what she always does when she thinks of her late husband. She puts on an Otis Redding album, and remembers.

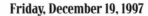

Friday, December 19, 1997

Big Man with a Big Heart
Chris Farley Was Madison's Own

The first time I met Chris Farley, he was scaring the heck out of a little kid.

It was an act, of course. It was a snowy December afternoon in 1993. Farley, dressed as Santa Claus, was rehearsing a sketch for *Saturday Night Live* on the eighth floor of Rockefeller Center in Manhattan.

"You're going to wake up Christmas morning," Farley bellowed at the boy, whose mother was being played by actress Sally Field, "and find your stocking full of JACK SQUAT! That's because there is no such thing as Santa Claus!"

Many Madisonians are feeling as if somebody took Christmas away Thursday. Chris Farley's death in Chicago made headlines around the world, but it hit hardest in the town he always regarded as home.

"Everyone is treating it like a Hollywood story," said Madison television producer John Roach, whose family and Farley's go back decades, Thursday night. "Here, it's a neighborhood story."

I wasn't a close friend of Chris's, but we got to know each other pretty well when I spent several days with him in New York for a magazine profile in 1993. He was already a star, at his peak on *Saturday Night Live* and beginning a movie career.

It didn't take long to realize Chris was different from most of the celebrities I had met through journalism. While

6

we were working out the logistics of my trip to New York, he called my house in Madison each evening to make sure everything was on the rails.

When I arrived in New York, accompanied by a mutual friend, U.S. Rep. Scott Klug, R-Madison, Farley introduced us to other cast members. He got us tickets to the show, and generally behaved like any other Edgewood High grad greeting pals from his old hometown. Wisconsin had just qualified for the Rose Bowl, and when Klug produced a Badger sweatshirt, Farley wore it during the show's finale.

He had us over to his apartment in Manhattan, which was packed with photos of Madison and his family. He talked about Edgewood: "I was disruptive in the classroom. A nun's nightmare."

Of attending college in Marquette and taking his first theater classes: "I came to think that was what I wanted to do. I was pretty sure I'd have trouble in the business world."

He talked about his big break, in August of 1990, when SNL producer Lorne Michaels flew to Chicago to catch Farley doing comedy at Second City. The next day Michaels called and invited Chris to his room at the Ritz-Carlton. "That's where he hired me," Farley recalled. "I was naked in his hotel room at the time."

For me, that line was typical of what Chris was like off-camera. He was funny, but in New York, and the times I was with him in the years that followed, I never saw the manic, out-of-control figure of pathos you'd occasionally read about in the tabloids.

Chris had his demons. When I asked him, during that New York visit, about the stories of excessive good-timing and general craziness, he took a deep breath.

"I had a lot of fear when I first moved to New York," he said. "I was away from home. I was on live television at 26. I was very scared. Maybe I was a little wild. But I've calmed down. People who get out of control fall by the wayside. I didn't want that to happen to me."

Surrounded by Reality

Another thing: During my New York stay, I happened to mention that a friend of mine in Madison had two young kids who were huge Chris Farley fans.

As soon as I said that, Farley was reaching for the telephone. When the kids came on the line he did a 10-minute rap as Matt Foley, motivational speaker—one of his most enduring characters.

The kids will remember that all their lives.

After my magazine piece was published, I saw Chris in Madison a few more times. His proud parents, Tom and Mary Anne Farley of Madison, were generally quick to let me know about the latest rung he'd climbed on the show business ladder.

Tom called this past June to let me know about a TV show, *Sports Bar*, that Chris would be appearing in along with his brothers, Kevin and John. Both of them were following in his comic footsteps. Tom and Mary Anne were proud of all the kids: The Farleys are a close family.

When Kevin acted as master of ceremonies at *Madison* magazine's "Best of Madison" party at the Edgewater a few years ago, Chris showed up. Naturally, he stole the show without trying. We had a room in the hotel and afterward, Chris, his mother, John Roach, my wife, and I went up to the room. We flipped on the television to find O.J. Simpson and Al Cowlings driving on a California freeway, pursued at low speed by police.

Between Roach and Chris, I'm afraid the jokes were not always in the best of taste. But they were hilarious. I'd pay a lot of money to have a tape of the talk in that room today.

Most of the news accounts following Chris's death Thursday afternoon have mentioned that John Belushi was his idol, but I'm not so sure. He told me one time that his hero "since I was a kid" was Bill Murray. Farley's favorite time on SNL was the week Murray returned as guest host. A sketch he'd written for Murray got on the show, and Kevin

8

and John Farley came to New York to watch.

Still, there was no denying his link with Belushi. Both were from the Midwest, with physicality at the core of their comedy. When Chris needed an agent, he went with Bernie Brillstein, who had represented Belushi.

At one point during my 1993 visit to New York, Chris took me into producer Lorne Michaels' office, a spacious suite one floor above the SNL studio. From Michaels' desk he picked up a framed photograph of the first-ever *Saturday Night Live* sketch, on October 11, 1975. It featured Belushi and actor Michael O'Donoghue.

"I know John's brother Jim," Chris said quietly. "I never knew John. I wish I had."

In years to come there will be young comedians who say they never knew Chris Farley, who died, as Belushi did, at 33. This much I know: If they had met him, they would have liked him. He was kind and gracious. Chris was from Madison, and of Madison. I feel rotten today, but I'm glad to have known him.

In the summer of 2005, Chris's brother Tom called me to say the family was flying to California—Chris was getting a star on the Hollywood Boulevard Walk of Fame.

1999

———

No Foretelling If He'd Get Refund

This all began six weeks ago with a call from an acquaintance, Madison attorney Mike Riley.

"I don't know if this is something for you or not," Riley said. "But it's a heckuva interesting story."

It was interesting, all right. As Riley told it, a friend of his had contacted Riley on behalf of a third party—a Madison man, Eddie, about 30 years of age, and employed in the service industry on the west side.

Eddie, which is not his real name for reasons that will be understandable momentarily, has a learning disability. He's had trouble coping with the death of his father within the past two years, and he readily admits he sometimes does not think straight.

In October, Riley said, Eddie went to visit a Madison psychic. But let's have Eddie himself pick up the story. I first met with him on January 25.

"I was brought up on spirituality, and I have always

looked for the truth," Eddie said. "I saw the psychic's sign from the road. I called up and made an appointment."

The appointment was in early October. The psychic, whom we'll call Jane, was about 40 and Middle Eastern. The visit lasted 45 minutes to an hour. Jane's rates were $30 for a half hour and $50 for an hour.

"She told me Satan was trying to control my life," Eddie said. Jane was talking to the angels, she said, and the angels wanted only the best for Eddie. "She explained my dad to a T," Eddie said. "That got me emotional. She said how my father was watching over me, and wanted Jane to help me."

At which point they made another appointment for the following week.

At that visit, Eddie said, Jane sold him some crystals and incense for $300. "This is going to protect you from Satan," she said. "Remember, Jesus loves you." The psychic also told Eddie not to tell anyone he had talked to her.

On Eddie's third visit, Jane told him his father had communicated something to her. "He wants this to happen," Jane said. What Eddie's deceased father wanted, Jane said, was for Jane to go to Africa, to retrieve what she called Eddie's "right spirit." Jane said she'd finance as much of the trip as she could, but she needed Eddie's help. She needed $6,700. Eddie said, "That's a lot of money." Jane said, "You're going to lose my help forever if you don't do this. Your father wants this to happen."

On October 22, Eddie went to the First Federal Savings branch on Gammon Road and purchased a cashier's check made out to Jane for $6,700. He then drove to her place of business and dropped it off. "You're doing the best thing possible for yourself," Jane said.

A week later, Eddie went back to the psychic, but this time an older woman, who also said her name was Jane, was there. She told Eddie that the younger Jane was gone for a little while, "taking care of your project."

For the next several weeks Eddie tried to reach the psychics by phone, without success. At one point in December, Eddie and a friend were in front of the psychic's business, which was closed, and they met a fire inspector who said, "Where are they? I need to do an inspection."

Eddie was wondering the same thing. He'd told a few friends what he'd done to, but not his new wife. He was sheepish, embarrassed, and when a friend told him, "God's word is free," he resolved to try to get his money back.

After we met early last week and Eddie told me his story, I called Glen Lloyd, an acquaintance in the Wisconsin Department of Agriculture, Trade and Consumer Protection. Lloyd heard me out and suggested I call the police, which I did. I swapped phone messages with a Madison police detective I know, Jim Grann, who in his message offered to help. As it turned out, he didn't get involved.

In the meantime, Eddie phoned. He had managed to get hold of Jane the elder, who said of young Jane: "She really wants to talk to you. But she's fasting for six weeks, and part of the fast is that she cannot speak."

Eddie persisted, and the elder Jane agreed to meet him, last Friday, at 5 p.m. He asked if I'd accompany him. We met a few minutes before 5 and Eddie was nervous but determined. He said he was going to say he had no problem paying the hourly rate, but that he wanted his money, the $6,700, back.

The elder Jane met us at her office. Eddie identified me only as a friend. Jane was very gracious, even when Eddie asked for his money back. "It's not right," he said. Jane explained that they had already spent more than the $6,700 on Eddie's project, but if he insisted, they'd return the money. But it was after 5 p.m. Could he come back on Monday?

I told Eddie not to get his hopes up, but we met Monday afternoon in the psychic's parking lot. He said he could go in alone and asked if I'd wait in my car. Five minutes passed. Ten. Twenty. And then Eddie walked out, with the biggest wad of cash I'd ever seen cupped in his hand. I could see the elder Jane through the glass of the door. Eddie got in my car. He was holding 250 $20 bills and 10 $100 bills—$6,000. "They said they'd try to get me the rest in a few weeks," Eddie said.

I followed him to the Hilldale First Federal, and Eddie deposited the $6,000. We shook hands. "Young Jane wants to talk to me," he said.

"You're not going to do something stupid, are you?"

"Never again," Eddie said, and drove off.

Monday night, I called Mike Riley. "No kidding?" the attorney said. "They gave him his money back? That's great!"

Eddie said he thought so, too.

Not long after this column ran, Jane the Psychic left town under the cover of darkness, owing several months rent to her University Avenue landlord.

═══════════

Tuesday, June 1, 1999

Era Ends for "Honorable Mother"

It had been 25 years, a quarter century of hard work and memories, many of them good, and so as it came to a close Friday evening, the tiny elderly woman who had been so strong for so long couldn't help it.

She wept.

Her name is Suey Wee Wong, and she is 82 and ageless. At the Chinese restaurant at 112 E. Mifflin Street—

named the Golden Dragon until recently, when it became the China Moon—she was known to the regular customers who became her friends as Bot Mo, or "honorable mother." Bot Mo had been the matriarch of the restaurant since it opened in 1974 and she was there Friday night when it closed, taking things off the walls and hugging an old customer who had come by one last time to say good-bye.

Her son, Suey Wong, a well-known and colorful Madison character about to embark on another career—in acupuncture—looked at his mom across the room, shook his head, and smiled. "She's not very good at letting go."

How do you let go of 25 years? The Golden Dragon was a family business, and that included employees and regular customers. The Wongs served a lot of lawyers and pols who worked in the capitol a half block away. The food was excellent but there was a bit of a culture clash because Bot Mo was a serious believer in ancient Chinese myths, and Suey, the talented but at times quixotic son, had firmly embraced Americana—the Daily Racing Form, for instance.

The Golden Dragon opened June 6, 1974. Bot Mo picked the day because the Git Sing Book of Oracles said it was a good day for a new venture.

It was more than a venture—it was an adventure. Regulars over the years included Paul Soglin—before, during and after his years as mayor—State Street businessman Dan Waisman, lawyers and lobbyists like Mike Brozek, Tony Varda, and Don Bruns, poker studs like Phil Hellmuth and all manner of legislators, bureaucrats, and other state capitol wildlife. Occasionally someone with abundant cash and no visible means of support could be found whispering into a telephone at the bar. I remember one guy in a loud golf sweater talking incessantly into a cell phone about point spreads and parlay cards. He hung up and got friendly with the woman eating fried rice next to him. "Where do you work?" he asked. "The IRS," she said.

Bot Mo took care of this crazy bunch. If you were a

regular she would have a free egg roll in front of you almost before you sat down. She often wanted to talk, which was a challenge because her English seemed limited to "Suey not here." She could be formidable. One time Bot Mo became convinced that another regular, the late journalist Jim Selk, was drinking too much. She produced a health drink—a vile-looking glass of green liquid that appeared to be filled with seaweed. Selk was not a man who liked being told what to do. He shook his head. Bot Mo insisted. Selk drank it down.

Her energy was amazing. One winter night Suey got a call at home from befuddled Sauk County authorities. A car was in the ditch off Highway 12. Everyone was OK, but it was three in the morning, a terrible snowstorm, and what were these elderly Chinese ladies doing out? "She'd been to Ho-Chunk," Suey said.

On Friday, when they heard it was the restaurant's last day, Tony Varda and some legislators who were having lunch bought Bot Mo a bunch of lottery tickets.

They should have let her buy them. Suey recalled a day in the 1980s when the entire family had gone to Forest Hill Cemetery to pay respects to Bot Mo's late husband. The weather was poor, and everyone had left except Bot Mo, who stood for a very long time in the rain while Suey waited in the car. "Mom, come on!"

Bot Mo turned and said, "Your father is giving me the lottery numbers." Finally, reluctantly, she got in the car. It was the Illinois lottery and she made Suey drive to South Beloit to buy the ticket. "She hit five of six," Suey said. "She won $3,800."

Was Bot Mo thrilled? Suey grinned. "She said if I hadn't rushed her, she would have hit all six and won millions."

2000

================

Billiards Duo Racks Up Memories

It's usually in the fall that Nancy Hart thinks about her old friend Rudolph Wanderone.

It was in October that Wanderone would invite Nancy and her husband, Gordon Hart, to his home in Dowell, Illinois—the southern part of the state known as "Little Egypt"—and offer them chocolate-covered strawberries from his refrigerator.

The first time was October 1965. The Harts had driven down from Stoughton, where they owned a small pool hall, because near Dowell, in Johnston City, Illinois (population 3,400), a man named George Jansco was putting on the World's All-Around Championships of billiards. It was a Super Bowl for pool players, and a gathering of some of the most colorful characters in any sport anywhere.

Gordon and Nancy met them all. Wanderone was built like a sofa and talked constantly. Until 1961 he had shot pool in obscurity, and if people called him anything it was New

York Fats. But that year a movie with Paul Newman and Jackie Gleason came out called *The Hustler*. Wanderone went into the theater and came out with a new name—"Minnesota Fats," which happened to be Gleason's name in the picture. "They stole my life," Wanderone said, and true or not, it was the end of New York Fats.

Nancy Hart of Stoughton would recall that despite what some of his detractors said, Fats could really shoot pool. And he was unsurpassed at getting a betting edge for himself. Most pool wagers are won before the balls are racked.

Other road legends showed up in Johnston City. There was Hubert "Daddy Warbucks" Cokes, a septuagenarian oilman who carried a shotgun with four barrels "to make up for my poor eyesight." Fats revered him.

The '65 tournament ran three weeks, and the Harts returned to Stoughton. But the high school moved, and their pool hall business wasn't that great. Gordon, who got his first pool cue at 12, began fooling around in the basement making cues himself. He used an ancient lathe and found he had a talent for it. The Harts bought an old motel on Syene Road off the Beltline in 1969 with the idea of making and selling cues for a living.

Meanwhile, every October, they returned to Johnston City for the world championships. It was addictive. There was laughter, big talk, and tall stories against a Gatling gun background of pool balls in collision. No one ever looked at a watch.

The fun ended, with the Harts in attendance, in 1972 when 50 federal agents with warrants and subpoenas knocked down the door. "Most of us were ordered to appear before a grand jury in East St. Louis," Nancy Hart recalled. All the loose cash had drawn the feds, and although nothing came of it, no fines or jail time, the Johnston City tournament was history.

Gordon and Nancy Hart came back to Madison and their fledgling cue business. They called it Viking Cue, and you might say it has done pretty well. Today they sell more than 1 million cues a year out of the expanded Syene Road space, and they are one of the top three in the world at what they do. A German collector just paid $10,000 for a Viking cue that Nancy said "was loaded with ivory."

Gordon supervises the making of the cues, and Nancy handles the business and promotion end. Recently, the bible of the pool industry, *Billiards Digest* magazine, polled industry insiders to establish the 10 most influential people, worldwide, in billiards. Nancy Hart ranked sixth, but if 100 people passed her at West Towne, probably not one would recognize her name.

That's OK with Nancy. She loves what she's doing. Now and again, she and Gordon and some longtime friends will sit and talk about those wild old days when Minnesota Fats loomed large in Johnston City. She says, "For color and excitement, nothing could match it."

═══════

Monday, April 17, 2000

Basketball Against the Big Guy

This was a Saturday near Thanksgiving last year, and Adam Carl was doing what he does most Saturdays: Getting his team set for a pickup basketball game at a Chicago gym on North Clark Street called the Gold Coast Multiplex.

Carl, 29, is a native of Northbrook and now works as a sales executive for an internet company in Chicago.

In the early '90s, Carl came to Madison to study political science at the UW, and he made the basketball team as a walk-on, serving as backup point guard to Tracy Webster. The UW coach then was Stu Jackson, and Carl was recalling

Sunday that they played a game against Dick Bennett, then
coaching UW–Green Bay.

Now Carl gets his basketball fix from the Saturday
games at the Gold Coast. There are a few real players in the
games—ex-Badger Sean Mason is a regular—but the play level
is mixed. The first guy Carl, who's a shade under 6 feet,
usually looks for is a big man, maybe 6 foot 6, named Tony,
who plays a physical game. You want him on your team. "I
don't like to lose," Carl said.

On that Saturday in November, Carl was in the gym
and thought he spotted Tony through a Plexiglas window,
bench-pressing some weights.

"I pounded on it and said, 'Let's go!'" Carl said. But
when the big man turned around, it wasn't Tony.

"I just sort of shrugged and said, 'Sorry, wrong guy,'"
Carl recalled.

Games at the Gold Coast are fast and furious, and if
your team loses, you sit for at least three games. Carl's team
had won a few in a row when he noticed the big guy from the
weight room come on the court for the next game. One gym
regular on the big man's team pointed at Carl and said,
"Guard him, he can shoot."

The big guy said, "Whatever."

He didn't guard Carl the first few times down, and Carl
made a jumper and a driving lay-up. The third time down, the
big guy switched to Carl, but didn't follow him out beyond the
three-point line, and Carl nailed a long one. "My shot's
actually gotten better over the years," he said.

Carl hit a couple more, and then on a drive he caught a
hand from his big opponent. "Foul," he said. The big man
looked at him. "Foul?" Then he laughed. "OK."

Carl's team won the game and kept playing. The big
guy sat down. He waited through three games. Carl didn't
hear it, but somebody told him later the big guy said, "I'm
going to shut that guy down."

Finally it was his turn again. Carl's team had kept

winning. And as Carl brought the ball down, he noticed the big man had come all the way up to the half-court line. "He was kind of tugging at the bottom of his shorts," Carl recalled, "and I looked at him and said to myself, 'I've seen him do that a hundred times.' He was shading me to the left. I knew I was in trouble."

Any basketball fan knows that look. It means Michael Jordan is getting serious. "I couldn't even get a shot off," Carl said of his second time around against the greatest player ever. "I mean, I've played with Michael Finley and held my own, but this was, well, Michael Jordan."

The next day, Sunday, Carl went back to the gym just to shoot around. It was almost empty, but Jordan was again in the weight room. He didn't come out, but when Carl got in the elevator to leave, Jordan stepped on. He grinned. "I spotted your weakness," he told Carl. "You can't finish when you go to your left."

Carl said, "No, I can't finish to my left against Michael Jordan." Jordan laughed. He came back to the gym the next several Saturdays. Once he even rented the gym on a Sunday and invited Carl and some of the better players to play a game with Jordan and his friends. But then, as must happen often in Jordan's orbit, word of his presence leaked, and one Saturday at the gym there were dozens of friends of friends who knew nothing of basketball and were there only to see Michael Jordan.

The big guy looked around, and smiled at Carl. "Too much riffraff," he said, and then he was gone.

Three years later I did another column that involved Jordan. A UW–Madison senior who caddied in Chicago in the summer got to carry Jordan's clubs when he played a round at Olympia Fields with Tiger Woods. Michael tipped $200—Tiger, $100.

===

Monday, July 31, 2000

A Mother's Life Now Seems So Brief

It hadn't hit home, the man thought, really hit home, until the social worker at the HospiceCare inpatient facility in Fitchburg said, "You know, some people pass the time at bedside working on the obituary."

"How long are we talking?" the man said.

The social worker, who had just talked to a nurse, said, "Days."

Well, the man thought, you can write an obituary. You've written enough of them. Usually it was someone famous he had known, a politician, perhaps, or a colorful bar owner. It's a bit different, the man thought, when the person dying is your mother.

So rather than write, he thought about this place, HospiceCare, where he had come so often in the past weeks. He knew he had never seen a medical facility like it. There was an aura of peace about it. Fine art prints by Diego Rivera and Russell Chatham hung on the walls, and outside, through the abundant windows, the trees always seemed to be swaying in the breeze.

The people of HospiceCare, the nurses, desk attendants and others, were unfailingly kind, compassionate, and—of equal importance—honest. The man knew he was not alone in wondering how they could do what they do, day after day.

It probably helped to keep a sense of humor. The man thought of the French writer and philosopher Voltaire, who was lucid as he lay on his deathbed. A friend had thought to

21

bring a priest. "Mr. Voltaire," the priest said, "would you like to denounce the devil?"

Voltaire peered up at him. "My good man," the philosopher said, "this is no time to be making new enemies."

Now at HospiceCare the man looked at the woman on the bed. She won't be making any funny cracks, he thought.

How do you summarize a life of eight decades, anyway? It seemed a long time, but now, looking back, it appeared to have passed in an instant.

If he were to write anything, he thought, he'd likely begin with her volunteer work. Not only because she spent so much time volunteering but because it would tell others much about her. How many days had she spent giving her time, freely, to Madison General Hospital, later Meriter, as well as Oakwood Village? If you added it up it was years. She won awards for that service, but she also gave in a less organized way to anyone with a moment of need.

She had many enduring friendships in her life, and they were with people of character and substance. She read more than anyone the man had ever known, and there was a time he wondered why she stuck with mysteries. Then he remembered it was she who first introduced him to the works of John D. MacDonald, Ross Macdonald, and Raymond Chandler, writers who will be read as long as people read books.

She had, at her core, an iron will. When her husband had a heart attack and had to quit smoking, she quit, too, after 40 years. She didn't use a patch or any nicotine gum. She just stopped.

She had four grandchildren and loved them very much. The second set was here in Madison, so she could spoil them almost daily, as a grandmother should.

The man knew if he was honest he would write that she was not perfect. She sometimes had trouble expressing her emotions to those closest to her. Those people likewise had trouble sharing their feelings with her. The man had lived long enough to know this did not make his family unique.

The cancer that had come earlier this year was quick and deadly, and to the surprise of no one she refused treatments. It was time.

Now the man's wife was in the room and it was the three of them and it was quiet. "I feel helpless," the man said at last. "I want to do something."

His wife said, "You could tell her you love her."

"It probably wouldn't register."

"Tell her you love her."

He did.

Wednesday, August 9, 2000

Detective Lulling a Great Character

Chuck Lulling was a cop before police work required sensitivity training.

A Madison native, Lulling joined the police force in 1949 and became a detective in 1960. He successfully closed more than 20 homicide cases, including some of the highest-profile crimes in Madison's last 30 years.

Lulling investigated the 1970 Sterling Hall bombing that killed researcher Robert Fassnacht. He recalled that as "two years out of my life." I once asked if the relatively light sentences given the bombers bothered him. "When you do your job, you can't tell the court how to do its job," he said. "I couldn't care less."

A decade later, Lulling headed the investigation that

resulted in the murder conviction of Barbara Hoffman. During the trial Lulling found someone who was convinced Hoffman would walk. Lulling—who said "there are occasions when I'll wager a coin"—offered a bet, and came away from the verdict $600 richer.

Betting on a murder trial was not out of character for the colorful Lulling. I got to know him a bit through a mutual friend, Jack McManus, the hugely successful and piratical Oregon attorney who frequently hired Lulling as a private eye after the detective quit the Madison police in 1978.

Lulling originally had planned to relax and do leather work. He was good enough to sell belts to a store in Arizona and holsters to police departments across the country. But he missed the action, and what gambler can't use a little extra cash at the end of the month? So he opened a P.I. practice. I met him early in that practice and liked him, much to the consternation of my defense attorney friends, some of whom felt Lulling occasionally crossed ethical lines in his zeal for his work. I'd like to think he didn't, but I've seen that line crossed on both sides, and as someone once said of Chicago politics, "We're not talking about beanbag."

Lulling liked the role of grizzled, world-weary, seen-it-all investigator. He had tattoos on his thick forearms, and he enjoyed a smoke and a drink, though by the time I met him he was trying to cut down. "My wife told me I can't drink it as fast as they make it," he said.

Once I was sitting in Lulling's "office"—really the study of his west side home—when the phone rang and a potential client was on the other end. I could hear the man's high-pitched voice. He was in Nashville and had been referred to Lulling.

"What do you need?" Lulling said.

It turned out the man's wife was in a Madison hotel room. Could Lulling go over and see what was up?

"It's $200 up front," the detective said.

The man from Nashville hung up. Lulling laughed.

24

"More than he wanted to invest in his wife," he said. A minute later, still thinking about the call, Lulling said, "I hate a case like that. I don't care who's sleeping with who. If they're not good enough to keep their wife interested, don't cry on my shoulder."

Another time I went along with Lulling when he had to interview a witness for a case he was working for McManus. He had a Silverado with all the gadgets, and as he slipped behind the wheel he donned dark sunglasses even though it was raining. Our destination was a police station in Sauk County. McManus' client was a jailer who had been roughed up while booking a suspect and was now suing the suspect for civil damages.

Lulling was interviewing a policewoman who had witnessed the altercation. It didn't go well. She objected to his tape recorder and said she hadn't really seen much.

Lulling thought it ironic that as a lifelong cop he didn't really get along with the police in his second career. "A private eye is a Monday morning quarterback," he said. "I second-guess everybody, including the police. I just go over all the details and everything that's been done so far. Some police are outright hostile. They're not good cops, and they're afraid to let me second-guess them."

I last talked to Lulling a few years ago. I had developed a theory—actually, it was *Rads* author Tom Bates' theory—that Leo Burt, the only Sterling Hall bomber still at large, was the Unabomber.

Lulling gave the kind of snort he reserved for rank amateurs. Well, I said, what *did* become of Burt? "I think he died and no one thought to tell us," he said.

Chuck Lulling died in Madison over the weekend, at 77, and I thought I should tell people.

Monday, August 28, 2000

The Mystery of Alfred Lawson—Who?

Los Angeles filmmaker Jim Newman, a Stevens Point native, came through Madison recently doing research for a documentary he's putting together on Alfred Lawson.

You've never heard of Lawson?

"Nobody has," Newman was saying Sunday. "That's one reason I want to do this."

What Newman, reached by telephone in Los Angeles, didn't want to do was talk publicly about his movie, since it's still a work in progress. Lawson's followers—who are still based in Wisconsin—are notoriously distrustful of the media. Newman said he had to respect that.

Newman was in Madison this summer to talk to UW–Madison Professor Barry Orton, who has an interest in Lawson and was referred to Newman by an Iowa writer, Lyell D. Henry, author of the 1991 book *Zig-Zag-and-Swirl: Alfred W. Lawson's Quest for Greatness*.

Still, the question remains: Who was Lawson, and why would he be of interest to authors and moviemakers?

It's a story that might begin in the dining room of Chicago's Blackstone Hotel on a late August day in 1919. It is noon, and three men from Milwaukee have come to town for lunch. One of them is Alfred Lawson. He is 50, though a *Chicago Evening Post* reporter thinks he looks 45—"a brisk sportsmanlike looking man just a little ahead of the times."

Lawson had arrived in Chicago in what the reporter called an "air giant"—an airliner built in Milwaukee by Lawson that seated 26 passengers, with a wingspan of 95

26

feet and a cost of $150,000. Over lunch at the Blackstone, Lawson said, "It's a shame we didn't think to bring some passengers." He had come on a whim. They had taken off from Milwaukee intending only to circle the city. Once in the air, Lawson said, "Let's drop down to Chicago." It took them 85 minutes.

Lawson had been lured to Milwaukee in 1917 by businessmen who liked the planes he was building in Green Bay. Born in London, Lawson played major league baseball in Boston and Pittsburgh before coming to Wisconsin.

Lawson saw himself as a visionary—in aviation and beyond. In 1916 he had written an editorial for *Aircraft* magazine in which he predicted a nonstop airline voyage across the Atlantic before 1930 (Charles Lindbergh did it in 1927), and said that prior to 1970, "air traffic will be practiced to such an extent that traffic rules of the air will have to be enforced (and) certain rights of way prescribed for different classes of air vehicles."

On May 8, 1921, Lawson was in a plane that took off from Milwaukee and crashed after hitting a tree and a telephone pole. He survived, but gravitated away from aviation toward economic theory and philosophy. He denounced ownership of money and property, wrote books, and founded the Lawsonian religion in 1948. He said that Lawsonomy "introduces penetrability and zig-zag-and-swirl movement with the key to perpetual law." Other ideas included dunking the head into cold water twice a day and sprinkling freshly cut grass on salads.

In 1943 Lawson set up the Des Moines University of Lawsonomy in that Iowa city, but in 1951 he bought 40 acres of farmland in Sturtevant, Wisconsin, on I-94 near Racine and the Illinois border. He moved the university there and sold the Iowa property.

By then he was in his 80s, and proving to have been a better forecaster of aviation's future than of the future of his religion. Lawson had claimed that by the year 2000 all races would accept the principles of Lawsonomy.

He died in a San Antonio, Texas, hotel room in 1954. He was 85, and no one in his organization would comment. The death certificate said it was a coronary occlusion. A Des Moines obit said Lawson had always refused questions about his personal life while stating Lawsonomy was "the knowledge of life and everything that pertains thereto."

In 1965, a *Milwaukee Journal* reporter knocked on the door of the Sturtevant university and found "one dedicated instructor, two staff members—and no student body."

Still, they persevere. There is a website—www.lawsonomy.org—and Newman, the California filmmaker, said the group has a booth at the Oshkosh air show every year. That's where Newman found them 15 years ago, and eventually got interested enough to embark on his documentary.

He has shot a lot of footage, but because he hopes for the continued cooperation of the remaining Lawsonomy believers, Newman didn't want to say much else. Thirty-five years ago they had invited the *Milwaukee Journal* reporter not to return by saying, "Truth and falsity do not mix."

That, then, is Alfred Lawson—as mysterious in death as he was in life.

Saturday, October 14, 2000

Picture Is Worth ... A Lot of Coincidences

In 1928, 40 years after she started her business, Martha Matilda Harper commissioned artist Ned Renold to paint her portrait.

It was to hang in a prestigious gallery, and people who saw it would know that this was a woman of large, even incredible, achievement. Harper had been sent away from home at age seven, worked for years as an indentured servant, yet somehow found the means to open a beauty salon in Rochester, New York, in 1888.

And not just any salon. It was far ahead of its time, with on-site day care and organic products. Harper invented the reclining shampoo chair. A visitor from Chicago was so taken with the salon that she demanded Harper open one in Chicago.

It was a big step that worked out pretty well. Today Harper is known as the inventor of the franchise concept—she ended with 500 salons, including one in Madison. She could afford to commission a portrait of herself.

Jane Plitt was talking about all this Tuesday on Jean Feraca's public radio show. Plitt, who lives in Rochester, was touring for her new book, *Martha Matilda Harper and the American Dream.*

Plitt was telling Feraca how she's working, with New York Rep. Louise Slaughter to get Harper on a postage stamp (Hillary Clinton is also a supporter of the idea). Plitt also mentioned Rochester's museum for Harper, and told how the 1928 portrait should be there but isn't. It was thrown in a dumpster and destroyed in 1995, she said.

Robin Cahill, mother of five and wife of Mineral Point artist David Cahill, happened to be listening to Feraca's show Tuesday. She heard the name Martha Matilda Harper, and her immediate reaction was: This can't be *my* Martha Harper.

Back in 1995, Cahill had been searching around for a good Father's Day present for her husband. In an antiques shop in Richland Center, she bought a portrait painting identified as "Martha Harper" and made a gift of it to her husband. The shop owner gave her a comb that said "Harper Method" along with the original photo the portrait was painted from. "I knew she owned a comb and brush factory, and that was it," Cahill said. "My kids call her Ma Harper because they think she looks like a gangster's mother."

As Plitt and Feraca continued, it dawned on Cahill that the portrait they were talking about was her portrait. "I called the show," Cahill said. "I said, 'Guess what? I look at Martha every morning.'"

Plitt was stunned. "If you could hear a jaw drop on the radio," Cahill said, "you would have."

No one is sure how the portrait ended up in a Richland Center antiques shop. In fact, Cahill isn't absolutely certain that's where she bought it—she thinks it was Richland Center.

The Rochester museum folks are "thrilled" with the discovery, Cahill said, and have asked permission to borrow it for a traveling exhibit they're planning on Harper in Washington, D.C. Cahill is leaning toward saying yes, and beyond that said, "I would part with it if it went to the right place." At this point no one is certain how much it is worth.

It is all a wild coincidence.

Cahill said she "almost didn't listen" to Feraca's show that day. Later, Cahill would realize an even greater coincidence, one that might make you wonder if there are any coincidences.

Back in 1995, when Cahill bought the portrait, she was pregnant. At that point, of course, she knew the woman in the portrait only as Martha Harper—she learned it was Martha Matilda Harper only this week.

Shortly after buying the portrait in 1995, Robin Cahill gave birth to a girl.

She and David named her Matilda.

Friday, December 8, 2000

Eisenberg: It's Great to Be Back

Nobody loved being a lawyer more than Don Eisenberg.

So when his phone rang in Florida early Thursday morning and Eisenberg learned that after 16 long years, the Wisconsin Supreme Court was reinstating his law license, of course he was pleased.

"Fantastic," he said.

When they first suspended his license, in 1984, Eisenberg was at the end of a decade-long run of high-profile criminal defenses that included big victories (a 1975 acquittal for UW–Madison professor Marion Brown on drug smuggling charges) and devastating losses (early '80s murder convictions for Barbara Hoffman and Lawrencia Bembenek).

Win or lose, Eisenberg played the high-rolling mouthpiece role to the hilt. He liked fast cars and first-class air travel and pushing all his chips onto the roulette table in Monte Carlo. He belittled prosecutors and fought with cops and swaggered through courthouses all over the country.

Eisenberg is 67 now, still a proud man, but the swagger is gone. He's a grandfather five times over, and while he's happy to have his law license back, he has moved on with his life. That includes fighting battles no jury can decide. Diagnosed with lymphoma several years ago, Eisenberg was in remission until just recently, and he's begun the painful chemotherapy treatments again. He's still going to work in his successful process-serving business in Orlando, but it's tough.

Over the years he was sometimes his own worst

enemy. He lost his license originally because of a conflict of interest in the Hoffman case. Eisenberg at the time was representing an all around bad actor—drugs, prostitution, gambling—named Sam Cerro. Cerro had a buddy, Grover Garrott, prepared to testify against Hoffman if the DA would give Cerro a break. It appeared a pretty clear conflict. If Garrott testified or didn't, either Cerro or Hoffman would be hurt. Could Eisenberg represent them both?

Eisenberg would always say he didn't see it, adding that Hoffman was aware of the situation and pleaded with him to keep her case.

But the Supreme Court pulled Eisenberg's law license for six months, and later extended it when they determined he had practiced law during his suspension.

Hanging over everything during this time was a federal grand jury investigation of Eisenberg that slowly was driving him crazy. I sat with Eisenberg in his office early in 1986 and he shook his head wearily. "They think I am a cocaine dealer," he said, "probably a heroin dealer, that I am a procurer for prostitution, and that I am a money launderer. And they're out to get me."

His eyes filled with tears and he added, "My whole world has crumbled. They're destroying me."

When the indictment came, it was for laundering $100,000 in cash for a drug client. Eisenberg hired Steve Hurley and Hurley won an acquittal, but the damage was done. With his loyal wife, Sandi, Eisenberg moved to Florida to start over.

In the next decade he continued to reapply for his law license, and the Wisconsin Supreme Court continued to turn him down. Until Thursday. Most in Madison's legal community were surprised but pleased when the news hit. By any measure, Eisenberg had done his penance.

He said Thursday he has no intention of moving back to Wisconsin. "Too cold," he said. He hopes to maybe work a few cases with his sons, Mark and Steve Eisenberg, who have a successful practice here. "That's the whole world," he said. "My sons and their families."

One of those sons, Steve, said Thursday that he hopes to list his dad as "of counsel" with the firm. "I think he'll come up and second chair for us occasionally," Steve said.

Steve knows better than anyone how much it means for his dad to call himself an attorney. "For 16 years he was told not to say that. Now he can."

2001

═══════════

It Was a Dark and Stormy Tale

There was a wedding in 1939 that brought her to Madison.

Her name was Jean Hilliker and she was one of the most beautiful women who ever hit town. A redhead. A year earlier, in 1938, she'd been voted the nation's "most charming redhead" in a contest sponsored by Elmo Beauty products. That took her to Los Angeles. She was 24 and didn't want to be a movie star, she said. But California was fun. She lived there and was murdered there.

Jean Hilliker had been born in Tunnel City, Wisconsin, near Tomah. She came back to Wisconsin, to Madison, in 1939 for the wedding of her sister, Leoda Hilliker, to Ed Wagner.

After the ceremony, Jean went back to Los Angeles. She got married to a man named Ellroy and in 1948 gave birth to a son named Lee Earle Ellroy. By the time the boy was ten, Jean was divorced and living in the L.A. suburb of El Monte. One night, while the boy was with his father, Jean went out for drinks. She stopped at a bar called the Desert Inn. It was June 21, 1958.

The next morning three Babe Ruth League baseball players going out to hit fly balls found Jean Hilliker's semi-nude body lying near the ball field. She'd been strangled.

Jean's sister Leoda and her husband Ed flew to California for Jean's funeral. Ed was composed, Leoda was distraught. They flew back to Wisconsin and told their daughter Janet, then age four, that Aunt Jean went to the store and got kidnapped. The police found her body the next morning. The crime was never solved.

Janet—the first cousin of the boy who was ten when his mother was murdered in 1958 —now lives in Cross Plains. She is in her 40s and her name is Janet Klock. Her husband, Brian Klock, works for the UW–Madison as a carpenter. We spoke Tuesday and the topic was her cousin, that little boy who lost his mother to such a heinous crime.

Janet said her mom and dad had tried hard to help the boy, but he lost his way after his mother's death. "My mom (Leoda) became custodian of her estate," Janet said. The boy would recall: "I conned coin out of Aunt Leoda (in Wisconsin). The 'I need dental work' pitch worked wonders." Eventually they lost touch. "We had no more contact after 1966 or so," Janet said. "He was living on the street in Los Angeles." The boy would later say he had lost himself in drugs and alcohol. He'd been in and out of jail.

Then, in 1996, a remarkable thing happened. A private investigator named Bill Stoner, a retired L.A. homicide detective, phoned the Klocks in Cross Plains and asked to speak to Janet. He was working for her first cousin, now a middle-aged man, to help him try to solve his mother Jean's homicide after all these years.

"I was really shook up," Janet said of the phone call. "We thought he was dead. The way we had last seen him, there didn't seem any way he could survive."

Stoner, the investigator, arranged for the man, who

had changed his first name to James, to meet Janet Klock. The two men flew from California to Madison. The Klocks came in from Cross Plains and met them at the airport. When James met Janet, he didn't recognize her. After all, it had been 30 years.

"But we're so happy he's back in our life," Janet said. "We've stayed in touch."

It has been an interesting few years for the Klocks. As Janet said Tuesday, "What we found out was that not only was he alive—he was famous." Very famous. Today James Ellroy is one of the best-known crime novelists in the world. His best-selling novels include *L.A. Confidential,* which was made into a hit movie. *Time* magazine has a profile of Ellroy in its current issue, and Tuesday's *New York Times* included a lengthy review of his new novel, *The Cold Six Thousand.*

The novel that put Ellroy on the map was *The Black Dahlia,* based on a sensational L.A. murder that was very similar to the murder of his own mother. Ellroy and Stoner never did solve that crime. The boy didn't find Jean Hilliker Ellroy's murderer. But he found some family in Cross Plains. James and Janet spoke just before the author left on a late April book tour to England and will meet again at a June book signing in either Milwaukee or Chicago.

"It had to be scary for him to find us," Janet said. There were ghosts, and 30 lost years. "But we're so glad he did."

Ellroy came through town a few years after this column appeared. I chatted with him in his suite at the Edgewater. He's as colorful in person as in print—big, intense, and opinionated.

===

Monday, June 25, 2001

The Classiest Guy in the Room

You should know that right until the end, he was the classiest guy in the room.

Tony Moe, who died here Saturday at 86, knew how to do it. Life, I mean. My dad couldn't hit a golf ball or start a charcoal grill, but he had an easy sophistication and a sense of what really matters in life that stayed with him until—well, how about a week ago today?

Last Monday afternoon we were in a meeting room at Middleton Village, where he was rehabilitating after a hospital stay in which we had almost lost him. There were eight therapists and nurses sitting with us—all female—and my dad was telling stories and jokes. He'd been there only two weeks but already they regarded him with great fondness.

Through all his medical woes—a heart attack 15 years ago, small strokes, and, most recently, a difficulty in eating and swallowing that had left him frail and weak—his wit never left him. Neither did his will to live. Last Monday, he actually seemed to be rallying. A nurse mentioned he had walked some 30 feet by himself. He whispered to me he had been looking for the bar.

He usually found what he was after. When he and my mom moved to Madison 40 years ago, they were looking for a nice place to raise their two kids. They had met in Sioux Falls and wanted to come back to the Midwest after years of city-hopping as my dad climbed the executive ladder at CBS Television.

Surrounded by Reality

I had been born in Connecticut while my dad commuted to Manhattan on the railroad. Eventually he decided a CBS vice presidency wasn't worth the commute. He came to Madison to manage WKOW-TV/Channel 27 in 1960 and wound up in the Wisconsin Broadcasters Hall of Fame. He oversaw the building of seven new television stations in this state—first with Channel 27, and later as executive director of the Wisconsin Education Communications Board.

His life in television took him interesting places. Oh, he loved to travel. Occasionally I got to go along. As a teen I saw *Follies* on Broadway and attended the 1971 U.S. Open golf tournament at Merion in Pennsylvania. My dad was on the ABC affiliate board of directors, which got us into the ABC tent at the Open. We shared a lunch table with Frank Gifford and the sportswriter Jim Murray.

Sometimes the famous came to him. He brought the original *Mod Squad* to Madison for a March of Dimes benefit his station was televising. Another time I remember coming home for lunch and finding Chet Huntley sitting in our living room. The legendary anchorman was part of a group that eventually bought Channel 27.

Being on that affiliate board was a great deal. It allowed my parents to see the world on the company nickel, and in those days ABC spared nothing in courting its affiliates. One of my dad's favorite stories came out of an affiliate board meeting in Puerto Rico. He was sitting around his hotel waiting to be picked up for a meeting when he struck up a conversation with a stranger who turned out to be a pretentious name-dropper. The man went on and on about himself and his importance until he finally ran out of gas. Then, right on cue, the public address system announced: "Mr. Moe, your helicopter is waiting." My dad just smiled and walked out to "his" helicopter.

In recent years most of his travel involved going to see my sister and her family in Michigan. He was so proud of them and their beautiful home on Lake Michigan. He was, of course, a doting granddad.

I can remember exactly the night I knew he wouldn't live forever. I was 24, he was 65, and we were walking a long way across the Coliseum parking lot to a Badger hockey game. It was freezing and the wind was ferocious. By instinct he started to walk in front, to block the wind, but it pushed him back into me. We kind of looked at each other and then I stepped in front. He had many, many good years after that, but I never forgot it.

At that meeting last Monday, all the therapists had given their reports. The mood was upbeat. The next day I would get a call that he had taken a bad turn, but for now everyone was pleased and we were looking for an exit line.

"Hey, Dad," I said. "Your helicopter is waiting."

He left smiling.

Monday, August 13, 2001

Coppola Disaster Unfolded Here

With the Friday opening in selected cities of *Apocalypse Now Redux*, Francis Coppola's reassembled Vietnam epic starring Marlon Brando and Martin Sheen, many critics took the opportunity to remember that the filming of the original 1979 movie was the most controversial, chaotic, and downright crazy shoot the flamboyant Coppola had ever overseen.

They were wrong.

The craziest shoot Francis Coppola ever presided over took place in downtown Madison—not long after the release of the original *Apocalypse,* as a matter of fact.

In a sense it all began when California Governor Jerry Brown tried to appoint the actress Jane Fonda to the California Arts Council. When she was rejected as too political, Brown turned to Coppola. The director agreed—it didn't amount to much beyond evaluating grant proposals—and the two got to know each other well enough that when Brown decided to challenge incumbent President Jimmy Carter for the 1980 Democratic nomination, he asked Coppola to create some TV ads.

Brown liked the commercials, but he needed to win a primary somewhere to jump-start his campaign. It was mid-March, and the early April Wisconsin primary looked like a possibility. Didn't Wisconsin favor mavericks?

Brown and Coppola got together and emerged from their bunker with the idea of producing a live 30-minute television show, originating in front of the Wisconsin capitol, that would be beamed into every television market in the state on the Friday night before election Tuesday. They would call it *The Shape of Things to Come,* the title of an H.G. Wells short story about the destruction of a society by war and its rebirth through technology.

A Brown staffer told the *Village Voice*, "I have no idea what he's going to do. All I know is that Coppola intends this thing to be one of the collector's items of his career."

Coppola came to Madison Wednesday, March 26—the show was scheduled for 7 p.m. the night of March 28. The director arrived with his wife, two sons, and Bill Graham, a rock music promoter.

That night Coppola spoke at West High School and explained that the centerpiece of the live program would be a high-resolution video system under development at his Zoetrope Studios in California. Utilizing an electronic chroma-key process, Coppola would flash images illustrating Brown's points onto a huge screen that was to be behind

Brown as he spoke outside the capitol.

The crew assembled Thursday afternoon in the capitol. A Channel 3 cameraman, John Gaska, had been hired by Coppola to be the man to cue Brown. That was a little more than 24 hours away. Gaska would remember that at their first meeting Coppola said, "We'll zoom in on Jerry and then a half dozen airplanes will fly right over the capitol!"

At which point a capitol police officer said, "No, sir, you can't do that. It would be too low and—"

"What!" Coppola screamed. "I don't care. We'll fly 'em right over the flagpole!"

That night—actually early Friday morning, about 3 a.m.—they tested all the hardware outside the capitol. A surprisingly large crowd was on hand, and as the lights blazed a helicopter came roaring around the dome and someone shouted, "Holy Jesus! Francis is going to napalm us!"

He didn't, but the next night he did a pretty good job on himself—and Brown. Coppola warmed up the crowd of 3,000 outside the capitol by saying they were about to participate in "an act of media piracy." But when Brown began speaking, the vaunted chroma-key technology misfired, and on eight TV stations around the state pieces of Brown's face appeared to be breaking off and sliding offscreen. Even when the images worked, they were bizarre. When Brown spoke about investing in new technologies, the screen behind him showed a Skylab astronaut doing somersaults in his underwear.

Later, the $450,000 production finally over, Brown paced a hallway in the Park Motor Inn and asked, "How did I look?" A staffer replied, "A little like Claude Rains in *The Invisible Man*."

On April 1, election day, Brown completed his disappearance. He got 12 percent of the vote in Wisconsin and dropped out of the race. Coppola had already fled Madison—tipping his Union Cab driver, Stuart Levitan, $50— leaving politics for the relative sanity of making movies.

===

Monday, November 19, 2001

"Snowball's" Story Is Madison's

She had never seen an obituary like it.

"No one knew his exact age," Marsha Stewart recalled. "Or his birthplace or if he had any surviving relatives. He had never had a Social Security number, nor had he paid any income taxes. I was amazed how anyone could be so outside the system."

Stewart is a financial consultant with Merrill Lynch in Madison. She came to Madison in the early '60s to go to school, and her dorm was across the street from the Rennebohm's drugstore at University and Park. That's where Stewart first saw John "Snowball" Riley.

It was later, after Riley had died and she had read his extraordinary obituary, that Stewart decided to try to learn more about the man who was a legend in Madison, albeit a legend shrouded in mystery.

Ten days ago, in a column about the singer-songwriter Utah Phillips, I mentioned that Phillips had been intrigued by Riley during earlier visits to Madison. Phillips had been having breakfast at a State Street cafe and noticed Riley outside washing windows. Now the singer was hoping to learn more about the man he had heard called Snowball. I wrote what I knew, which wasn't much.

Stewart saw the column and got in touch. After Riley's

death, she spent a year trying to learn more about him. "I had thought about writing a book," Stewart said. She interviewed many people in Madison and still has 200 hours of audiotapes. A treasure. Those tapes tell not only about Riley but about the experience of being black in this city in the last century.

Stewart interviewed people like Odell and Hazel Taliaferro. Odell worked in the UW chemistry department, but his real work was fighting bigotry. He led a sit-in at the capitol over fair housing and helped pass the city's equal opportunities ordinance in 1963.

The Taliaferros told Stewart that Riley came to Madison in 1923 or 1924, on a train. Harry Allison met Riley about that time. Allison never had a big job but he was an educated man. He knew Latin and German and had a large house on the corner of Desmond Court and Murray Street where blacks new to town often stayed. Duke Ellington stayed there because no Madison hotel would rent him a room.

Allison told Stewart that Riley said he came from a place near St. Louis. Others laughed when Riley said he was from Finland. Well, there's a small town in Mississippi, 90 miles from St. Louis, called Finley. Stewart thinks that may be his hometown.

For a long time in Madison, Riley lived above the Greenbush neighborhood tavern owned by Zack and Maxine Trotter. Zack Trotter had moved to Madison from Georgia in 1913 and taken a job as a waiter at the Park Hotel. He worked hard and opened his own place. In 1960, when urban renewal came to the West Washington-Park Street-Regent Street triangle area, Trotter was forced to sell his bar. He found a place farther down Park Street, only to have the neighbors petition against him. A white bar owner, meanwhile, relocated—near a school—with no problem at all.

In her interviews, Stewart learned that Riley was a

hard worker (construction in the early days), a sharp dresser, a lover of trains, horses, sports, and women. Riley had some trouble once on a trip to Chicago and wound up in jail. Race entered into it, people said, and when he came back—Zack Trotter had gone down to help—something about him had changed. He didn't smile as much. Riley became a fixture on State Street, washing windows, getting by day to day. He still loved clothes. Stewart said the owner of McNeil and Purnell (a State Street clothier) told her Riley came in and bought a $25 silk tie on layaway, paying a quarter every so often until it was his.

A man named Muhamed Mousouf Aziz did a pen and ink drawing of Riley that Meuer Art turned into a postcard that sold 2,500 copies in the first three months of 1976.

Riley had died the previous year, in October 1975. He was buried in Forest Hills. The Reverend Joseph Washington, the son of a slave and for close to 40 years the pastor of Mount Zion Baptist Church, gave the eulogy.

Before his own death in 1986—at 95—the Reverend Washington told Marsha Stewart that after Riley's death, the funeral director at Joyce had approached him with 19 dollar bills.

"What's this?" Washington said. The funeral director said John Riley had insisted they be given to the minister at his funeral. While Stewart was interviewing him, Washington produced a roll of crumpled, mutilated bills. They were Riley's, and of course Washington had kept them, in memory of a man who, while he lived outside the system, lived large.

Tuesday, November 27, 2001

Playboy Dresses Down UW Myth

We should be proud of ourselves.

The readers of this space and the guy whose mug appears above it made enough of a racket last summer that *Playboy* magazine, in the January issue on sale next week, addresses once and for all the question of whether UW–Madison ever was ranked by *Playboy* as the No. 1 party school in the United States.

Or whether the magazine ever did a party school ranking but left out UW because it didn't want to rank "pros with amateurs."

This all started in August when the Princeton Review came out with a list of the nation's top 20 party colleges, and UW–Madison ranked ninth.

I wrote a column saying that the publicity from the Princeton survey would almost certainly lead people in Madison to talk about the notorious *Playboy* ranking. The *Playboy* story is as much a part of Madison lore as the 1948 *Life* magazine cover on Madison as the best place in America to live, Otis Redding's plane crash, or a handful of others.

The only problem, I suggested after talking to *Playboy* spokesperson Elizabeth Norris, was that it appeared never to have been published.

The ranking was a myth.

Well, the responses rained down, dozens and dozens, mostly from now middle-aged guys who swore they had read the story. For some it seemed to loom as large as the Kennedy assassination, as they remembered exactly where they were when they read it.

On Monday I obtained an advance copy of the January issue of *Playboy*. It's not the Pentagon Papers, but you take your scoops where you can get them.

On page 47, the *"Playboy* Advisor" (actually a *Playboy* staffer named Chip Rowe) prints a question from "S.D." from Madison.

S.D. is actually a Madison resident named Steve Donovan.

Here is Donovan's question as it appears in *Playboy*: "This past summer a *Playboy* representative told the *Capital Times* that your magazine had never ranked the University of Wisconsin as the nation's top party school. The problem is that many alumni, myself included, remember reading this in the magazine more than 30 years ago. Can the Advisor help straighten this out?"

And now—drum roll, please—here is the definitive response by the all-knowing *Playboy* Advisor, from the January issue:

"Technically, we've ranked party schools only once, in January 1987, and UW does not appear on the list. (It's posted at Playboy.com/faq.) What you remember is our September 1968 issue, in which we listed UW as the most permissive campus in a sample of 25 universities. We also called it the party school, primarily because it served beer in the student union. We repeated the exercise in October 1976, naming UCLA tops in campus action. Each month we receive letters from students or graduates of any number of schools, insisting that *Playboy* named their campus as party central. Or they heard their school had been disqualified because we didn't rank professionals."

Allow me, your humble servant, to interrupt here and say the next passage of the Advisor's response should interest the many readers who heroically volunteered to go through every issue of *Playboy* page by page in an effort to find an answer.

The Advisor concludes: "The first person who can produce evidence of any ranking besides those mentioned above earns a degree in Playboyology—and we'll throw in a subscription to the textbook."

That's it. Didn't happen. No ranking. No pros vs. amateurs. Just that 1968 issue and a *Playboy* nod to UW–Madison as "the party school."

If you are still confused, what can I tell you? That's what you get for reading the articles.

The Wisconsin Alumni Association magazine, On Wisconsin, *picked up on this column, and I subsequently heard from people all over the world who swore they had read the "pros vs. amateurs" article in* Playboy. *They did not.*

≡≡≡

Tuesday, December 18, 2001

Ex-Showgirl Still Quite a Show

"I dated Joe DiMaggio for two years," Gregg Dodge was saying Sunday.

"But that story? In the book? It never happened."

The book, a DiMaggio biography by Richard Ben Cramer, was a recent best-seller.

"I'll tell you why it never happened," Dodge said. "Until I married Horace Dodge, I never drank."

I first read the story that never happened more than a year ago. Reading it began an odyssey that ended, finally, on Sunday, when I dialed a Palm Beach phone number and a woman answered.

47

Surrounded by Reality

"Hello."

"Gregg Dodge?"

The woman's voice, not unfriendly, said, "Who is calling?"

"I'm a reporter in Madison, Wisconsin."

There was a pause. "Really? I'm from Beloit."

"I know."

I knew, all right. Last January I wrote a column about my unsuccessful search for Beloit native Gregg Sherwood Dodge Moran, a former Miss Wisconsin who moved to New York, became a showgirl, dated celebrities like DiMaggio and Dean Martin, graced the cover of *TV Guide*, acted in motion pictures, married money—most notably automotive heir Horace Dodge Jr.—spent all the money and more, moved to Palm Beach, and, in 1990, was the subject of a lengthy profile in a magazine called *Fame* titled "The Artful Dodge: She's gone from vast wealth and a fairy tale existence to a stint in the Palm Beach county jail. But the unsinkable Gregg Dodge has persevered to become Palm Beach's prime example of how to stay afloat amid a sea of bitchy women."

On Sunday Gregg Dodge said: "How did you find me? My number isn't listed."

My search had taken me to the Academy of Motion Picture Arts and Sciences in Beverly Hills. A librarian named Kristine Krueger located a file of newspaper clippings from the *Los Angeles Herald Examiner* and *Los Angeles Times* and the "Milestones" section of *Time* magazine, faded clips that told an extraordinary tale.

Her name was really Dora Mae Fjelstad. Her father, Mons J. Fjelstad, was a carpenter, and on Sunday she remembered him. "My dad played checkers with Governor Kohler," she said.

She graduated from Beloit High School and went to New York with a modeling contract. She flopped. She returned to Beloit, changed her hair color and her name, and went back. "I moved back as a platinum blonde and was an

48

instant success," Dodge said in 1990. "I had modeling jobs, more than 150 magazine covers, TV shows, films, even Broadway shows."

The *TV Guide* cover was November 5, 1949, and the magazine said: "Her luck changed with her hair color and she became the highest-paid showgirl in the country."

Her personal life, however, was tumultuous. In 1950 the *Beloit Daily News* reported that Gregg's second husband, a ticket manager for the New York Yankees, had been indicted on charges of grand larceny. She divorced him and married Horace Dodge, heir to $57 million. In August 1958 the *L.A. Herald Examiner* wrote that Gregg was intoxicated and arrested for battery to a police officer when the cop pulled her and Chicago gossip columnist Irv Kupcinet to the curb of La Cienega Boulevard in Los Angeles. Gregg's explanation: "We were looking for Frank Sinatra somewhere, but missed him."

After Dodge died during divorce proceedings (leaving Gregg with $11 million from a pre-nup), Gregg married Daniel Moran, 12 years her junior, whom she met when he was a private bodyguard for Barbara Rockefeller. The *Janesville Gazette* would later report the following: "(Gregg and Moran) embarked on a 13-year spending spree that included $25,000-a-night parties and round-the-world flights in a private jet, which exhausted the $11 million."

Moran died in 1978 and Gregg landed in Palm Beach, where she has stayed. "I don't really want to talk about all that," she said Sunday. "I don't know you are who you say you are, do I?"

Still, she was happy to chat. She remembered Dean Martin fondly: "We were great friends." It was a half century ago. In those days, she said, Martin had a room at the Bryant Hotel at Broadway and 54th in New York. "He had a roommate—Sonny King," she said. King was an ex-boxer turned singer.

She said she never pounded drunkenly on DiMaggio's

hotel room door, as reported by Cramer in his book. We talked a bit about the Gore-Bush election fiasco, which peaked in her backyard, and she said she is close to a deal that will have her as publisher of an "international" magazine.

What would she be now—78? Maybe 79. I wasn't about to ask, though she couldn't have been nicer. I got her phone number Sunday from her grandson, Johnny Dodge, whose number I got from a newspaper reporter in Palm Beach.

A decade ago Gregg had said, "I spit fire. I always have, and I always will." I thought she was wonderful.

2002

===

Monday, March 4, 2002

Two Murder Cases Eerily Similar

The day that little girl went missing in San Diego I thought about my friend Mark Lemberger.

Then late last week, when the worst was confirmed in the current case and seven-year-old Danielle van Dam was found dead, a San Diego man told the *New York Times*, "We're in an age where a girl can be in her bedroom and not be safe in a good neighborhood. It's just unfathomable."

It may be unfathomable—but it has nothing to do with the age. A chillingly similar crime happened here 89 years ago.

Both crimes involved seven-year-old girls asleep in their family home. Both disappeared from their beds in the middle of the night. Both were found later, away from the home, murdered. In both cases, a male neighbor was charged with the crime.

Though it generated considerable national publicity at the time—10,000 inches of newspaper copy, by one estimation—the Madison kidnapping and murder had been largely forgotten by the 1980s. Mark Lemberger was a computer salesman in Columbia, South Carolina, when his mother sent him a news clipping occasioned by an anniversary of the Madison murder. The victim was named Annie Lemberger. She would have been Mark's aunt. His dad was born five years after Annie died.

"The story absolutely picked me up by the lapels," he later told a South Carolina newspaper. He took a leave of absence and came to Madison, determined to write a book about the case, which was officially listed as unsolved. We met in the late '80s when Mark was contracted to write some historical articles for me at *Madison* magazine.

"You've heard of Annie Lemberger?" he asked.

I had not. Mark told me a little about the case and I asked how the research was going.

"I'm four years into my two-year leave of absence," he said.

It had become an obsession. It haunted him. On Sunday I asked Mark if the reports from San Diego had reminded him of Annie. "Oh gosh, yes," he said. "And I'll tell you something else. Thank goodness for DNA, or those parents out there could have become suspects, just like the Lembergers did."

Mark was referring to a bizarre twist in the Lemberger case. Annie had disappeared from her family's home in the Greenbush neighborhood the night of September 6, 1911. She was found floating in Lake Monona Bay four days later— "bruised about the head," according to a *State Journal* article at the time. Just as in the current San Diego case, a neighbor was fingered for the crime. Unlike David Westerfield, the man arrested in San Diego, James "Dogskin" Johnson, quickly confessed to the murder and was convicted. He subsequently recanted his confession, and a decade later, an attorney named Ole Stolen took up Johnson's cause and produced a witness, a Lemberger neighbor named Mae Sorenson, who said Annie's brother told her that Martin Lemberger, Annie's dad, had beat her to death with a beer bottle.

Martin—Mark's grandfather—was charged with the crime. But when Sorenson failed a polygraph—one of the first times the machine was ever used—she admitted having been paid to lie. Martin was set free, but so was Johnson, by order of the governor, having served 10 years of his sentence.

For his book, eventually published in 1993 as *Crime of Magnitude,* Mark Lemberger gave the case a thorough reinvestigation. He located a forensic background check of Johnson that fit the sexual predator profile. He concluded that Johnson had murdered Annie. Last summer, the History Channel interviewed Mark for a series of programs called *Forensic Firsts,* focusing on the polygraph.

With his book in print, Lemberger moved to the San Francisco area. He donated a copy to a local library and one day a woman called him and said, "Why didn't the little dog in the Lemberger house bark?" They chatted a bit and the author suggested he might fill her in over coffee.

He not only told her the answer, he married her. Mark and Penny now have a daughter and are living in York, South Carolina.

====

Monday, March 18, 2002

Shake the Hand of Max Hurwitz

He wore a beret, sold apples and sandwiches from a pushcart on campus, and somehow, right after selling his last apple, he built an amazing house with an indoor swimming pool just off University Avenue.

Surrounded by Reality

Max Hurwitz was a Madison original.

This started last week with a note from a reader wanting information on a man named Max who peddled apples in Madison and used to hand out a picture of himself shaking hands with John F. Kennedy. "Shake the hand of the man who shook the hand of Jack Kennedy," he would say, and there was the picture to prove it.

It was as if one day in the 1940s Hurwitz just materialized behind the pushcart at the bottom of Bascom Hill. His background was sketchy. "Max," someone asked, years later, "with all your years on campus, did you ever attend classes?"

Max grinned. "No one will ever know."

He always seemed to be smiling. Why not? Life was pretty good, and when it wasn't, or things got boring, Max would stir the pot. Like the time he pushed his cart from State Street to the west end of campus and started selling hot dogs along with apples. Great idea! That first day, he sold hundreds of hot dogs. Of course he did. It was a football Saturday and Max was on Breese Terrace getting to all those hungry fans before they got into Camp Randall, which made him popular with everyone except the "W" Club, which was selling hot dogs inside.

Max was arrested. This was 1949. Peddling without a license, selling in a restricted area—11 counts in all. The case bounced from court to court, and even though the police chief, Bruce Weatherly, testified against him, Max won. Judge Roy Proctor dismissed the charges. They nabbed Max again in 1952—same charges. That time it dragged on until 1956, when Max's lawyer got the city attorney to sign a stipulation dropping the whole thing once and for all. Max's attorney? Roland Day, who wound up as chief justice of the Wisconsin Supreme Court.

Back in the '40s, when he began selling apples, Max and his wife, Arlyne, bought a modest house on Blackhawk Avenue—just off University Avenue east of Midvale. They also bought the lot next to it and, over the years, other real estate as they were able. Let others earn 2 percent with a savings account. His pushcart wars taught Max property trumped a passbook any day.

One of Max's acquisitions was a rooming house on Butler Street that he called The Regent. He bought the building in 1962 and registered the name with the secretary of state. That came in handy a few years later when the new owners of an eight-story, $1.5 million apartment building serving 900 students a block from Camp Randall on Regent Street opened amid much publicity calling itself The Regent. Of course, Max filed suit, asking $40,000 damages. He wound up settling for $200. By then it was 1965 and he had bigger fish to fry.

As an anniversary present to themselves, Max and Arlyne had decided to build a new home on the lot adjacent to their house on Blackhawk. Max being Max, it wouldn't be just any home. He and the designer-builder, Herb DeLevie, did most of it themselves. It took 75 tons of stone and included seven levels of rooms, a 14-foot fireplace, and an indoor swimming pool.

"I'm glad I live next door," Arlyne said. "It's been fascinating to watch." Word got out, and in 1967 Max had an open house. Hundreds showed up for a tour, and when they got to the terrace, in a place of honor was the pushcart that had started it all.

Max enjoyed working with his hands, and not long after his house was completed, he was in the capitol building downtown when he noticed workers removing all the grillwork from a number of elevator doors. "What's up?" Max asked. "Progress," he was told. Max got busy and talked the powers that be into giving him the old elevators, which had been installed around 1910. He wound up with 19 doors and 17 cage sections, and when someone asked what he was going to do with them, Max said, "Maybe have them for breakfast. Nothing like a little grillwork to sharpen the teeth."

When he died in 1986, he was recalled as an apple peddler with a puckish sense of humor. He was that and more. Those who remember like to think that somewhere, once in a while, Jack Kennedy is asking people to shake the hand of the man who shook the hand of Max Hurwitz.

≡≡≡

Saturday, May 4, 2002

Some Derby: No Racing Form

One of the great semi-guilty pleasures of my life was spending many hours during Kentucky Derby week perusing a fine newspaper called the *Daily Racing Form*.

I say "was" because today you can't buy a racing form in Madison. That sorry news was confirmed Friday when I called the form's 800 number.

"The closest place to you looks to be Delavan," the operator said.

It was never exactly easy to find a form here. I first got hooked on the horses in the summer of 1989, when Paul Soglin, then starting his second lengthy stint as Madison's mayor, invited a group of us down to the grand reopening of the Arlington International Racecourse northwest of Chicago. The track had burned to the ground in 1985, and a rich guy named Richard Duchossois spent $160 million to rebuild it and then some.

Driving down in the van that day, Soglin was deep in concentration and making pencil notes in a tabloid paper— the *Daily Racing Form*.

As I learned—this was my first trip to a racetrack—the form is a bible for horse players because it contains charts showing the past performances of the horses that will be racing that day. To the uninitiated it appears to be written in some strange code, but once you master the lingo, it's great fun to absorb the minutiae of the form and use that intelligence to try to bet on a winner.

The form, which started publishing in 1894, also has features and opinion columns—and a proper sense of perspective. By that I mean the form does not ignore news outside the racing world. For instance, a front page top-line headline in the form might read, "Secretariat Wins Triple Crown." On an inside page, there would be a few paragraphs in a box under a small header: "World Peace Close at Hand."

When George Plimpton interviewed Ernest Hemingway for his "art of fiction" series in the *Paris Review*, Hemingway pointed to the *Daily Racing Form* and said, "There you will find the true art of fiction."

It used to be there were two outlets in Madison carrying the form. Snappy's Place on King Street went down first, on the last day of 1992. John and Ida Wilson ran Snappy's in the shadow of the capitol for about 40 years. It was a great place to gossip, buy out-of-town papers like the form, and see which legislators liked looking at dirty magazines.

When Snappy's closed, racing buffs went to the other side of the square, to Pic-a-Book on State Street. But owner Dan Waisman started having trouble getting distributors to stock the *Daily Racing Form*. For a period of time Soglin had to go to the Badger Bus station every morning, pick up a bundle of forms, and deliver them to Pic-a-Book—a triumph of constituent relations, at least until Pic-a-Book, too, closed in the winter of 2000.

During Kentucky Derby week, the form puts out a special edition that you could usually get either Wednesday or Thursday. The proper technique for studying that edition was to have sharpened pencils, a table with lots of room for a pot of coffee, "minor" papers like the *New York Times* and *USA*

Today, and space for friends who might drop by.

It was nice to be in a public place like Suey Wong's Golden Dragon restaurant or Marsh Shapiro's Nitty Gritty—each a serious student of the ponies—because you could trade banter with other aficionados who were certain they knew who would win that year's Derby. You could also hear the woeful tales of losing bets that horse players take a perverse joy in relating. Marsh would tell about the horse he bet on that had a heart attack 10 yards from the finish line, and Suey would come back with one about a horse with a six-length lead that hit the mile pole on the rail and wound up jumping the track.

At which point someone would say, "You know Damon Runyon's greatest story? It's called 'All Horse Players Die Broke.'"

When I called Friday, the *Daily Racing Form* operator said, "You can find us online, you know."

You can, but it's not the same. They want a credit card for the past performance charts. And no friends or colorful characters are likely to drop by your computer terminal.

As it is, I will be in Delavan this afternoon, at the dog track, where I won't be surprised to see Soglin and the others. It's time my 10-year-old son learned the true art of fiction.

═══════

Monday, May 20, 2002

A Good Con Story Makes a Day

Talk about coincidences.

One day last week I was reading a review of Ricky Jay's new one-man Broadway show, *Ricky Jay—On the Stem,* directed by David Mamet, when Bronson La Follette phoned and said, "Do you remember Pappy Fry?"

If you've seen any of Mamet's movies about con men—*House of Games, The Spanish Prisoner,* and, most recently, *Heist*—you would recognize Jay, who acted in all of them.

But Jay is probably best known as a magician and authority on cons. He recently published a book titled *Jay's Journal of Anomalies: Conjurers, Cheats, Hustlers, Hoaxsters, Pranksters, Jokesters, Imposters, Pretenders, Side-Show Showmen, Armless Calligraphers, Mechanical Marvels, Popular Entertainments.*

Jay's current one-man show—the stem in the title refers to Broadway—is also a celebration of the shady side of show business and the art of the con. It's one of the toughest tickets to get in New York.

Which must mean I'm not alone in having always been fascinated by con artists. So much of politics, religion, and so-called legitimate business is about trying to put something over on the public that it's almost refreshing to come across an unpretentious and unabashed hustler like Pappy Fry.

There is also something to the old adage that you can't con a totally honest man. As one of Pappy Fry's victims—Pappy would have called him an investor—said on the witness stand in Madison, "I guess I was like everybody else. I hoped to get something for nothing."

After Bronson La Follette—who knows my affinity for colorful characters and Madison lore—called last week, I traded the Ricky Jay review for an envelope of yellowed newspaper clips and was soon under the spell of the story of Clark "Pappy" Fry, a Necedah farmer who claimed to have a secret formula, involving steam, that would create energy and render gasoline and other fuels obsolete.

It was a ridiculous notion, so of course Fry had people standing in line to give him their money.

Surrounded by Reality

Once it became evident that Fry had no magic machine and the matter wound up in court, some of the best legal minds in Wisconsin and indeed the Midwest found themselves involved.

Fry went to trial in January 1961. The eccentric federal judge in Madison, Patrick T. Stone, interrupted the trial and had a TV wheeled into the courtroom so he and everyone else could watch the inauguration of John F. Kennedy. That wasn't all Stone did. During Fry's original trial, Stone asked more than 1,200 questions from the bench and repeatedly ridiculed Fry, his attorney Willard Stafford, and various witnesses.

Stone asked one of Fry's victims how he happened to have so much extra money to invest. "I'm a bachelor," the man replied. "You better get married," Stone said. "A wife would have advised you to hang onto your money."

After Fry was convicted, Chicago lawyer Prentiss Marshall—later to become a federal judge himself—argued that Stone's behavior wrongly affected the jury. An appeals court threw out the conviction, and the case wound up back in Madison in 1962.

This time, Fry's attorney was Richard Cates, who would become one of Madison's best-known trial lawyers and work in Washington on the case for impeachment against Richard Nixon. The prosecutor was U.S. Attorney Nat Heffernan, who ended his career as chief justice of the Wisconsin Supreme Court. Throw in Pappy and his energy machine, and what a trial that might have been. Alas, Cates and Heffernan reached a settlement—the government dropped nine counts in return for Pappy's guilty plea on one count of mailing an unregistered security.

Cates gave a passionate argument for clemency, but a new judge, William Juergens from Illinois, sentenced Pappy to five years in prison. He died in a federal hospital in Missouri in 1964.

Pappy was 73. He never copped to having done

anything wrong, and maybe he really believed that given enough money, his invention was possible. Given enough money, what isn't? After the conviction, reporters asked Pappy for comment. "It's ridiculous," he said, and promptly excused himself to use the pay phone. Somewhere out there was somebody with $10,000 to make his bail.

I got an e-mail from Ricky Jay after this column ran, asking for more information on Pappy Fry. Maybe we'll read about Pappy in one of Jay's upcoming books.

Friday, June 28, 2002

Editor Gets Autograph the Hard Way

This was Thursday afternoon. A day like any other day in the no-nonsense business of reporting the news.

I was sitting around waiting to hear which legislator would be indicted next, or whether U.S. Judge John Shabaz was considering the death penalty for unpaid parking tickets, when the phone rang.

It was a cell phone call, and the static was terrible, but a voice was shouting. "Dave Zweifel just got bit by a (unintelligible) and he's OK but (unintelligible) and it was on TV!"

The line went dead.

Someone in the newsroom asked who was on the phone. I said, "It was a bad connection but I think someone said our editor just got bit by a vampire bat and it was televised."

Surrounded by Reality

"What?!"

"Maybe he'll call back."

The phone rang again. There was still a lot of static, but I could make out the voice of my old friend Al Zins. When I met Al he was working for Joel Skornicka in the mayor's office. Now he operates a successful public relations agency in Madison.

Al was shouting over the static. "Zweifel just got bit by Sammy Sosa! We think he's going to be OK."

The line went dead again.

Somebody came up to me. "Did you say Zweifel got bit by a bat?"

"That's what I thought at first. Zins was calling from a cell phone, and it was hard to hear. But the weird thing is, when he called back it sounded like he said that Zweifel didn't get bit by a bat. He got bit by Sammy Sosa!"

"He won't wash for a month."

That was a reference to Zweifel's well-known love of baseball in general and the Chicago Cubs in particular.

I sat there hoping the phone would ring again and tried to reason it out. I knew that every year Zins hosts a group of Madisonians at a Chicago Cubs game at Wrigley Field. A few years ago he invited me—I couldn't make it, too busy typing—with a group that included former governor Tony Earl, assembly minority leader Wally Kunicki, and Monona mayor Tom Metcalfe.

Thursday afternoon, the Cubs were playing the Cincinnati Reds at Wrigley.

My phone rang yet again.

There was more static but I could hear Zins shouting: "He's OK! He has an ice pack in one hand and a beer in the other!" Zins paused and shouted again: "Sosa just brought him over an autographed bat!"

At that moment *Capital Times* contributor John Oncken walked into the newsroom and said he had been listening to Cubs announcer Ron Santo on WGN radio in his car. "Santo said Sosa just hit somebody with a broken bat. He's blaming the bat companies. They don't make them like they used to."

"That was Zweifel he hit."

"What?!"

"Never mind."

But yes. On Thursday the annual Al Zins pilgrimage to Wrigley Field included Metcalfe, *State Journal* editorial writers Tom Still and Chuck Martin, and the *Capital Times'* editor. And at one point Sosa, the future Hall of Famer, cracked a bat swinging at a pitch, and part of the bat flew into the box seats and winged Zweifel.

The second best part of this story is that Zweifel is OK. The best part is that I got a column out of it.

Saturday, July 27, 2002

The Sinner Sprang the Preacher

Accused terrorist Zacarias Moussaoui's refusal to cooperate with his own attorneys is reminiscent of one of the more bizarre episodes in Madison's occasionally bizarre past.

In this instance, a man refused to come out of the Dane County Jail even though his bail had been paid.

It's a story that involved some of the city's most colorful and notorious characters of the 1970s and beyond—a Baptist minister, Reverend Wayne Dillabaugh; nude dance club owners Al and Tom Reichenberger; a couple of free-spirited attorneys, Eddie Ben Elson and Jack McManus; and public officials including district attorney Jim Doyle (now attorney general and a candidate for governor), Judge Bill

Eich, and Sheriff Bill Ferris.

Dillabaugh, minister at the Northport Baptist Church, was accused of misdemeanor battery for excessively spanking a five-year-old boy in September 1977.

On December 15, 1977, Dillabaugh was arraigned at the City-County Building and refused to either sign a signature bond or pay the $200 cash bail set by Judge Eich. Dillabaugh spent that night in jail.

Now at this point it needs to be said that Dillabaugh had been making a lot of noise around this time about the evils of the Reichenbergers' downtown nude dance club, the Dangle Lounge.

On hearing Dillabaugh was in jail, Al Reichenberger, calling on his good sense of humor and flair for the dramatic, had a brainstorm. "I thought," Reichenberger was recalling this week, "why not have the Dangle pay Dillabaugh's bail?"

As luck would have it, as Reichenberger strolled across the capitol square on that Thursday, who should he run into but Edward Ben Elson, a lawyer with his own abundant humor and gift for the outrageous. Of course the two knew each other. Elson had once announced his candidacy for Dane County district attorney in the nude on the stage of the Dangle. His campaign slogan: "Only obey good laws."

On this day in December 1977, Elson smiled at Reichenberger and said, "What's shaking?"

Reichenberger explained his mission. "What a great idea!" Elson said. "I'll represent you. No fee, of course."

The two proceeded to the jail. Up the elevator and out the door to the bail counter. Reichenberger handed over the $200. The jailer's response is lost to history, but when the prisoner was brought out and the circumstances of his release explained, a loud wail was heard behind the wall. Reichenberger recalled: "It was Dillabaugh and he was saying, 'Oh my god! No!'"

At which point Eddie called in: "Don't worry! We'll get

you out!"

Dillabaugh refused to leave. He called the bail "funny money."

Elson, though, was just getting started. He filed motions with the court insisting that if Dillabaugh refused to leave jail, he should be charged room and board.

"Actually, double room and board," Reichenberger recalled. "Eddie said Dillabaugh ate twice as much as anyone else."

Ferris, the sheriff, sought a legal opinion from district attorney Doyle, but Doyle said he couldn't get involved because his office was prosecuting the spanking incident. Ferris finally went to Dane County corporation counsel Glenn Henry, who said he would research the matter.

While Henry was researching, both Doyle and Judge Eich said informally that they believed release was required when bail had been posted. But on Friday—with Dillabaugh having spent two nights in jail and hundreds of supporters beginning to bus in from across the country—Henry came back with a decision saying Dillabaugh could decline the bail.

Judge William Buenzli then ordered him released anyway, with no bail posted. As it happened, the Dangle was just opening for business for the early evening crowd. Dillabaugh and his supporters walked down to the Dangle and held a rally outside. It was quite a spectacle. "Biggest night we ever had," Reichenberger said later.

In June 1978, courtroom gladiator Jack McManus won an acquittal for Dillabaugh on the battery charges. The controversial minister eventually moved to Pennsylvania, but not before sending a poinsettia plant over to the jail: "Sorry for any personal inconvenience. Pastor Dillabaugh."

Saturday, September 7, 2002

Poet Is a Stranger in His Own Land

Somebody once said there is nobody richer than a dead artist. If you watch the action at the New York auction houses, you know what I mean. Dying has its disadvantages, but for artists at least, it's a good career move.

Which brings us to the great Madison poet John Tuschen and the strange case of the $250 book of poems.

The other day Tuschen stopped into a local used bookstore. Because of my fondness for secondhand book stores, I will spare naming the store in the hope they were just having a bad day.

While in the store, Tuschen was pleasantly surprised to see one of his books in prominent view in a display case.

For all his talent and international reputation as a poet, Tuschen has not published a lot of volumes of poetry or made much money from the ones that did find print. Named Madison's poet laureate by Mayor Paul Soglin in 1977—a title he held until voluntarily passing it on a couple of years ago—Tuschen lives in modest digs on State Street, occasionally giving a reading and reminding people that we have an artist in our midst. In July 1999, a major online poetry magazine, *Poetic Voices*, published a 7,000-word essay lauding Tuschen.

The book Tuschen found at the Madison used bookstore is titled *Tuschenetrics: Poems from a cloth room and Paris*. It was printed in 1974—a total of 500 copies, some in Madison and some in Berkeley, California. "It sold well in Berkeley and San Francisco," Tuschen was saying Friday.

When the book came out in 1974, it cost $2.50. But in

the used book display case, *Tuschenetrics* was priced at $250. The poet was stunned when he noticed the price tag. He asked a clerk, "Is that book signed?"

"I don't think so."

"I'll sign it for $50," Tuschen said.

On Friday the poet explained: "If they sell it for $250, I get nothing. So I thought maybe I could get something for it."

The clerk did not believe he was the author.

"You don't think that's my book?" Tuschen said.

"You don't look like Mr. Tuschen," she said.

"I didn't have any ID," Tuschen said. "She just didn't believe I was me."

That night Tuschen related the story to his friend Sandy Von Lienen, a much-anthologized poet who lives in Mapleton, Illinois. Von Lienen has read with Tuschen here at Mother Fool's and has great love and respect for his poetry. Armed with the knowledge Tuschen had provided, she called the Madison bookstore.

At first the store said they didn't have any books by Tuschen. Von Lienen hinted that they might check the display case—saying Tuschen was a local poet—and the clerk came up with *Tuschenetrics.*

Von Lienen asked, "How much is it?"

The clerk: "Two hundred and fifty dollars."

Von Lienen: "What! Why?"

The clerk: "Well, it's an old book."

Von Lienen: "Is it signed? Maybe that's it. Did the author sign it?"

The clerk: "No, it's not signed."

Von Lienen: "Maybe the poet died or something."

The clerk: "I really don't know. It seems to me he died. Let me check." A minute passed and the clerk came back. "No one knows if the poet is still alive or not. They said he's local, though."

Von Lienen, who really would like to buy the book,

asked if there was any chance the price might come down. "It's an older book, out of print, so it will probably never be reduced," said the clerk. "They'll just keep it in the display case."

Tuschen found it all pretty funny, but Von Lienen did not. She told me, "To have this caliber of poet living in Madison, and have him go in a bookstore, ask about his book, and basically be laughed out of the store for claiming to be the author—it's terrible."

Maybe Tuschen can get a poem out of the experience. That's something no dead poet could do, anyway.

Alas, in August 2005, John Tuschen joined the ranks of deceased poets. He was 55.

═══════════

Tuesday, October 22, 2002

Tip of the Hat to a Great Journalist

Last week, when I heard that Tom Fitzpatrick had died, I did the only thing that seemed appropriate. I went home early, got down my copy of his collected columns, and took it someplace to have a quiet beer. Fitz was gone, but the columns were still wonderful company.

He died in June, and for a while last week I wondered how I missed it. Now I know. His death was barely mentioned, even in Chicago, where for several years he wrote the best newspaper column in that great newspaper city—the best column, I should say, by someone not named Mike Royko.

I never met Fitzpatrick, but read someone long

enough and you can feel like you know him. In the case of Tom Fitzpatrick, you came to know a tough kid from New York City who went to New Mexico on an athletic scholarship, dropped out, and wound up at Kent State, where a journalism professor told him he had no future in the profession.

His first newspaper jobs were in Ohio. Eventually he moved to Chicago, where by 1968 he had been on and off four different papers. "By that time," Fitzpatrick later observed, "I had created such an impression that I was describing myself on job applications as a freelance writer."

Then one night, probably in the Billy Goat Tavern, Fitzpatrick ran into Jim Hoge, the editor of the *Chicago Sun-Times* and an occasional player of long shots.

"Would you like a job?" Hoge said.

"Yes," Fitzpatrick said.

"Can you stay sober?"

"Reasonably so."

He was reasonably sober the night of October 8, 1969, when the city desk assigned him to cover the antiwar demonstration that eventually became known as the Days of Rage. Fitzpatrick, who worked off his hangovers by jogging, was in good enough shape to run for miles with the kids and the police and then, when it was over, run to the *Sun-Times* building and begin to type against a hard deadline of 20 minutes. When the clock ticked past the deadline, Hoge strolled over and said, "Let it run. Take whatever you need."

Fitzpatrick's piece on the riot began: "Bad Marvin had been standing in front of the fire he had made of the Lincoln Park bench for 30 minutes, shouting to everyone in the crowd and warning them how bad he was."

That story and others led Hoge to give Fitzpatrick a column, "Fitz," that ran five times a week near the front of the paper. His gritty prose and willingness to take an unpopular position got Fitzpatrick noticed, but what really iced it was that when he became a columnist, he didn't stop being a reporter.

When the bomb went off at the UW's Sterling Hall in 1970, Fitzpatrick was in Madison before noon. He wound up on the front porch of a home here, talking quietly with Gerard Fassnacht, who had driven all morning, too, from South Bend, Indiana. Gerard's son, Robert Fassnacht, had been killed in the blast. While his grandson, Christopher Fassnacht, played nearby (it was Christopher's third birthday), Gerard talked about his dead son winning a Westinghouse scholarship in high school: "Robert was the first boy in South Bend to win one, and when the telegram came his sister opened it. Robert, who was always modest, couldn't believe he had actually won."

That column, and another with a Madison dateline, are included in the one book Fitzpatrick ever published, *Fitz: All Together Now*, a collection of his *Sun-Times* writing. On Monday I checked alibris.com, the excellent online bookstore, and it had 13 copies for sale, all for under $20.

After Chicago, Fitz went to Arizona, where he worked for both the *Arizona Republic* and the *Phoenix New Times*. In between, in the mid-80s, he returned briefly to the *Sun-Times*. Like a lot of journalists, he didn't always manage his personal life as well as his sentences. A magazine profile of him in Arizona spoke of empty bottles and unpaid parking tickets. The same piece said there may never have been a tougher reporter.

When he died in Phoenix this summer, of lung cancer at 75, Fitzpatrick had been out of circulation a while, and the obits were few. I asked Jim Romenesko—who runs a great media news website—about it last week, and Jim said that while he'd had a few tributes to Fitz up on the site, current events had phased them off.

Well, that's the newspaper business. Tom Fitzpatrick knew it, and he knew the best part of it, too, like the day in 1970 when, not yet a columnist, he answered his phone at the *Sun-Times* and for once the official-sounding voice on the other end wasn't a bill collector. Hardly.

They were calling to tell him his Days of Rage piece had won a Pulitzer prize.

═══════

Friday, November 22, 2002

Bobby Fischer, the FBI, and Us

In J. Edgar Hoover's America, even paranoids had enemies.

When Bobby Fischer, the young and troubled chess genius, went to Moscow for a match in 1958, Hoover's FBI had already been tracking his mother for 16 years. Regina Fischer spoke eight languages and heard voices in all of them, according to a psychiatrist who pronounced her paranoid in 1943.

Regina's FBI file grew to 750 pages and it is that file, recently declassified, that eventually led two Philadelphia reporters to an archive in the Wisconsin Historical Society here, and the startling discovery, revealed in archived letters, that Bobby Fischer's father was likely not German biophysicist Hans-Gerhardt Fischer, as had been widely believed.

"It is quite a tale," Harry Miller, the Historical Society's senior reference archivist, was saying Thursday.

The documents archived in Madison are the papers of Peter Nemenyi, a civil rights activist who died in June at 75. We need to keep reminding ourselves that much of the history of the civil rights movement is living and breathing at the campus end of State Street. In the early 1960s the Historical Society director, Les Fischel, began aggressively soliciting civil rights and social action materials, until now it seems unusual when anything important doesn't come here. Not only do we have the papers of Daisy Bates, mentor to the "Little Rock Nine" heroes of desegregation, but here too is the rock that went through Bates' living room window when it was publicized she was helping the young black students. There is much more.

The Bobby Fischer connection in Peter Nemenyi's papers has to do with Paul Nemenyi, Peter's father. Fischer, after all these years, continues to fascinate and repel. The December issue of the *Atlantic Monthly* has a 10,000-word opus titled "Bobby Fischer's Pathetic Endgame," which indicates Fischer has become a recluse given to occasional lunatic rants on a radio station in the Philippines.

That behavior was hinted at in his most famous match, in Iceland in 1972, against Soviet champion Boris Spassky. After losing the first game Fischer blamed the lighting, the audience, and the high polish of the chessboard, eventually demanding that the second game be played in a Ping-Pong room off the main hall. At that, Spassky blew up, too, claiming Fischer was using an electronic device to spook him. In the end Fischer won the match.

It was spectacular theater, and even when he quit tournament chess Fischer remained famous for being famous, a condition proved irreversible by Ivana Trump and the cast of *Hollywood Squares*. Fischer's notoriety meant the *Philadelphia Inquirer* was interested in Fischer's mother's FBI file, which became available when Regina died in 1997. Reporters Peter Nicholas and Clea Benson got it through a Freedom of Information Act request, and when they started reading about Regina Fischer's Hungarian friend, Paul Nemenyi, they got in touch with Miller at the Wisconsin Historical Society.

Hoover's FBI thought Nemenyi was a communist. He appeared on their radar after Bobby Fischer went to Moscow in 1958 at age 15. Fischer was the precocious U.S. chess champion, and FBI agents monitored the trip closely, since they'd been snooping on his mother since 1942. According to Sunday's *Philadelphia Inquirer*, "Agents made it their business to find out who Fischer's father was."

The FBI was never certain, but Sunday, drawing on the letters archived in Madison, the *Inquirer* made the case for Paul Nemenyi. On Bobby's 1943 birth certificate, Gerhardt Fischer is listed as the father, and Gerhardt and Regina didn't divorce until 1945. But they had separated years earlier, and Regina came to the United States in 1939. Gerhardt never did.

The FBI files say Regina and Nemenyi met in the United States in 1942. Bobby was born a year later. In one letter after Paul Nemenyi's death in 1952, Peter wrote to a New York physician, "I take it you know that Paul was Bobby Fischer's father." The Historical Society also has a letter from Regina Fischer to Peter, after Paul's death, asking Peter "to let me know if Paul left anything for Bobby."

In the letter Regina mentioned Bobby's "torn shoes." Four years later, the name Bobby Fischer was known around the world. His half-brother Peter Nemenyi's life as a foot soldier for social justice never made headlines. He just did quiet good works wherever he went. Nemenyi's papers came to the Historical Society in 1975, but he was still at it until last summer, when he died, in modest circumstances and on his own terms, in North Carolina. The Raleigh paper had a sweet obit titled "Requiem for a social conscience." It didn't mention Bobby Fischer.

Wednesday, December 18, 2002

Can't Judge a Book by Its Owner

Tuesday morning I was over by the newspapers' shared library and there was George Hesselberg, making nice again.

"They arrest you yet?" he asked.

Hesselberg, the longtime *State Journal* columnist, had phoned me Monday to say he found a striking resemblance between my column picture in that day's paper and the surveillance camera photo of a bank robber that ran on Page 3.

He was enjoying his joke and that is typical of George. He is friendly. We get along. But now I know why he has been nice to me. He is consumed by guilt, as he should be.

Let me explain.

A few years ago I wrote a book called *The World of Mike Royko*, and part of that world is Mike's brother, Bob Royko, who lives in Madison and is an executive in the beer and wine business. Like most people not in the book business, Bob did not know that the author of a book receives only between six and 10 free copies of his book. While we were still negotiating with the publisher, Bob said, "Doug and I each get 100 free copies."

The publisher very much wanted this book, the first biography of Chicago's most famous newspaper columnist, and readily agreed to Bob's request.

One day about 10 boxes of books showed up in my driveway. Not long after that, I brought a book to the newspaper and walked it across to the *State Journal*, where I set it on the desk of my friend and fellow columnist, the previously mentioned Mr. Hesselberg. It seemed like a classy gesture. Inside I wrote, "For George—Who knows what this is all about."

If you haven't tried to fill a regular space in the paper several times a week, you can only guess what it is all about. As John Kass of the *Chicago Tribune* wrote in his introduction to my Royko book, the space gets hungry quick.

So a few years ago I gave a free book with a nice note to my friend George.

Later on Monday, the very day Hesselberg called to laugh about my resemblance to a bank robber, I found myself in the Frugal Muse, a fine used bookstore out on Mineral Point Road. I was looking for a copy of Jimmy Breslin's memoir, *I Want to Thank My Brain for Remembering Me*. In the book, Breslin reflects on his life as he gets ready for brain surgery. It also details the operation itself, performed in Phoenix by a renowned brain surgeon, Robert Spetzler. Not long ago I gave my copy of Breslin's book to the renowned Madison neurosurgeon, Manucher Javid, now retired, who I'm pleased to say told me he enjoyed it tremendously.

Anyway, I was in the journalism section of the Frugal Muse, looking for the Breslin, and there was a copy of my Royko book. I had not looked at it for months so I pulled it off the shelf and began to page through. That's when I saw it:

"For George—Who knows what this is all about."

Well, well. This was not quite as strange a sensation as another friend, the great Madison poet John Tuschen, recently experienced at another Madison used bookstore when he saw one of his old poetry books for sale for $250; when inquiries were made as to why it was so much, word came back that the poet was dead. It gets stranger. After I wrote a column about Tuschen and the $250 book, a columnist in the *Decatur Daily* newspaper in Alabama picked up on it and in a published item transferred Tuschen, the book, and the store to Madison, Alabama. Tuschen sent me the item. "Apparently I am dead in Wisconsin but living in Alabama," he said.

I mentioned earlier that my pal Hesselberg should feel guilty about unloading my gift to him at a secondhand bookstore. But who knows what really happened? You know how those *State Journal* types are. Maybe when I put it on his desk somebody swiped it. Probably Sunny Schubert. It was late fall, as I remember. Sunny might have taken it home, wrapped it, and given it to her husband and editorial writing colleague, Chuck Martin, for Christmas. Then when Chuck opened it to read, he noticed the inscription: "For George— Who knows what this is all about." Chuck would think, "Not only does my wife not know what this is all about, she doesn't know my name." So he took the book out to the Frugal Muse.

It might have happened that way. Or not. Maybe someday soon we'll read the answer in the *Decatur Daily*.

━━━━━━━━

Monday, December 30, 2002

Sen. McGuire? Might Have Been

Of course Al McGuire never went into politics. Just thinking about the possibility brings to mind something Art Buchwald wrote when Richard Nixon said he had always wanted to play sports but was "never heavy enough to make the team."

"I always wanted to get into politics," Buchwald wrote, "but I was never light enough to make the team."

Al McGuire, the free-spirited Marquette basketball coach who lives again in the pages of a new book by Milwaukee journalist Tom Kertscher, was never light enough for politics. But that didn't stop Lee Dreyfus from trying. This story comes courtesy of Bill Kraus, who rode shotgun during Dreyfus' four-year run as governor from 1978 to 1982. One day in 1979, Dreyfus invited McGuire to break bread at the governor's mansion in Maple Bluff. Al was riding high off his 1977 national championship. McGuire had wept on the bench after the Warriors won the NCAA title and then walked away from coaching. Providing eclectic commentary for games on TV had kept his name in front of the public, and now at lunch Dreyfus had a proposition.

"Why don't you run for the Senate in 1980?"

Gaylord Nelson was up for reelection. Dreyfus figured that if an unknown Stevens Point academic like himself could be governor, maybe a widely known basketball coach could be senator.

McGuire was not interested but Dreyfus persisted. It was, Kraus said later, great fun to watch and listen. "These two con men spent a wonderful hour trying to outcon each other," he said. Finally McGuire mentioned Billy Carter, a rogue whose antics at the time were causing grief for his brother, President Jimmy Carter.

"Governor," McGuire said, "I have a brother who makes Billy seem like Jimmy."

"Let's eat," Dreyfus said, and the McGuire candidacy was tabled.

Of all the headliners and legends who have passed through the state in my quarter century as a reporter, the one I most wish I had met and didn't is Al McGuire. Kertscher's book, just published by the Madison-based University of Wisconsin Press, helps fill the void. *Cracked Sidewalks and French Pastry* brings together more than 100 colorful McGuire quotations and dozens of photographs from his life on and off the basketball floor.

What was it about McGuire? The easy answer is that he was a basketball version of Yogi Berra, the catcher famous for descriptions like this one of a shadowy corner of Yankee

Stadium: "It gets late early out there." Or a restaurant: "It's so crowded nobody goes there." But Berra's lines, undeniably funny, began to sound scripted, probably because they were. McGuire was nothing if not spontaneous. He shot from the heart. As a consequence his aphorisms are less witty and more enduring.

Kertscher's book got a great national bump on Christmas Day when Frank Deford, the distinguished *Sports Illustrated* writer, made it the subject of his weekly National Public Radio commentary. Deford listed a few of his favorite McGuire bon mots: "I like seashells and balloons, ribbons and medals, bare feet and wet grass." Another: "I just put on a cocktail dress and go to work. My assistants are the ones who do the real work." And: "Sports is a coffee break." Deford's favorite: "When you bring flowers home to your wife and say there's no reason . . . there's a reason."

When McGuire lay dying of a blood disorder in a Milwaukee area hospice in January 2001, the best New York tabloid journalists, including Jimmy Breslin and Mike Lupica, came to pay their respects. McGuire had a tabloid flair. He came off the New York streets, and the "cracked sidewalks" of Kertscher's title refers to the tough neighborhoods where Al later found his best players. (French pastry refers to a not-so-tough opponent.)

When word of his illness leaked, I spoke with an acquaintance of mine who was one of McGuire's closest friends. Today Max McGowan is a highly successful marketing executive in Chicago, but in the late 1960s McGowan was, at 22, sports information director for Marquette. He learned much from McGuire and grew to love him.

Always there was laughter. McGowan recalled the time when a prestigious amateur basketball organization asked them to nominate the toughest opponent Marquette ever faced: "We listed the referee who fouled Dean Meminger out of the NCAA tournament in 1971."

2003

═══

Son of Pilot Thanks City for Its Generosity

Clark Stull left Madison when he was three months old. He's 44 now, and a successful chiropractor in Macon, Georgia. He has never been back to Madison, and he has never stopped thinking about it.

"The people in Madison will never know how much they have meant to me," Stull was saying Friday by telephone from Macon. "Words really can't express it. Without them, I couldn't have gone to college."

This is a story that starts with a young Air Force pilot and his wife moving to Madison in the fall of 1957. Gerald Stull was a civil engineering graduate of Texas A&M. His wife, Alice, gave birth to their first child, George Clark Stull, in February 1958. The Stulls weren't sure whether Gerald was going to make the Air Force a career or return to engineering.

Surrounded by Reality

The question became tragically moot the afternoon of May 5, 1958, when, on a routine training flight, the engine on Lt. Stull's $2 million F-102A fighter plane failed, and he crashed into Lake Monona just west of Olbrich Park. Witnesses and investigators called Stull, who died in the crash, a hero for the way he maneuvered to keep the disabled plane from hitting homes along Lakeland Avenue.

A resident on Lakeland, Joseph Butler, saw the plane and froze, convinced, he said later, that it could not miss his home. "I had the thought that my wife inside wouldn't even know what hit her."

Butler's neighbor, talking about Stull's heroism, said, "We sure owe that boy plenty."

As it happened, the city would soon begin making good on the debt. A week after the crash Alice Stull packed up her three-month-old son and went to live with her parents in Valdosta, Georgia. Before leaving Madison, she said, "This was in the back of my mind all the time. Pilots' wives live with it in their hearts."

In Valdosta, a trust fund in the name of the Stulls' son was established at the Citizens and Southern National Bank. The terms of the trust were that the money would be used for the boy's college or other higher education expenses. Checks from Madison began arriving almost immediately.

On February 5, 1973, the boy's 15th birthday, the *Wisconsin State Journal* published a small article saying that the trust fund had grown to around $9,500 and that Clark, as the boy liked to be called, played baseball and the acoustic guitar and had made the honor roll at school. When he turned 18 the trust fund allowed him to enroll and complete college.

"I wound up at Valdosta State College," Clark Stull said Friday. He lived in Atlanta for a time and is now in Macon. His mother, he said, is still living in Valdosta.

Stull said he would someday like to visit Madison, to see the lake where his dad died and to thank the city for its generosity in the wake of the tragedy. He pointed out that come this May, it will be 45 years since the plane crash.

"I think about him all the time," Stull said. "The newspaper clippings from the Madison papers are really the only history of him I have. My mother has a scrapbook."

He continued: "I make comparisons, you know? He was 26 when he died. When I was 26 I was just starting my practice. Now he would probably be retired."

The most famous airplane crash into Lake Monona was, of course, on December 10, 1967, when musician Otis Redding's plane bound for Madison from Cleveland went down on a cold and foggy afternoon not too far from where Stull's plane had crashed a decade earlier. The crash killed Redding, the pilot, and several members of Redding's band. It was only after I finished my conversation with Clark Stull on Friday that it dawned on me what a coincidence it was that Stull now lives in Macon, which was also Redding's hometown.

It must have also dawned on Stull, because a little while later my phone rang. "Clark Stull here again," he said. "I'd like to ask you something. I have never known for certain if the lake where my dad died—is that the same lake where Otis Redding crashed?"

"It is the same lake."

"I know Otis' widow," Stull said. "I'm going to call her. I never knew."

He paused for a moment and said, "What a small world. The other day they put up a memorial statue of Otis here in Macon. It's less than a block from my office."

≡≡≡≡≡

Tuesday, January 14, 2003

Roll Call: TP Museum Resurrected

The world-famous Madison Museum of Bathroom Tissue today exists in a garage in Elgin, Illinois.

It seems worth pointing out since a new edition of an old book has resurrected the museum and whoever is living in Carol Kolb's old apartment at 305 N. Hamilton Street might wonder why rolls of toilet paper from all over the world are showing up in the mailbox.

It dawns on me that some background is in order.

Kolb was a 24-year-old nurse's aide at Badger Prairie Health Care Center in Verona in March 1997 when 15 minutes of fame were thrust upon her by *Time* magazine. That month the venerable magazine founded by Henry Luce devoted a story to unusual museums, and somehow the magazine uncovered Kolb's isthmus apartment.

It had all started in 1994 when Kolb and her roommates were taking care of their thirst in a tavern outside Madison. It dawned on one of them that the apartment was out of toilet paper, and subsequently an emergency roll was liberated from the rural tavern. The kids began thinking it would be amusing to collect rolls from other, more exotic locales, and they spread the word among their friends.

By 1997 and the *Time* article, Kolb was calling herself the curator of a museum that boasted 3,000 rolls of toilet paper from places like Mount Rushmore, Lambeau Field, Ellis Island, the Alamo, and the Indianapolis Motor Speedway. To others it may have looked like John Belushi's frat room in

Animal House, but to Kolb it was a museum.

A reporter asked Kolb, "Is this museum a joke?"

"Certainly not," came the reply. "It's kind of a tribute to the common man."

Of course she was serious. If there is any doubt, just consider what Kolb is doing for a living these days. She's senior editor of *The Onion* in New York City. That's where I found her Monday.

I explained to Kolb that there was an article in a Vancouver newspaper over the weekend about this new book, *Offbeat Museums*, by Saul Rubin (Black Dog and Leventhal Publishers), which mentions the Madison Museum of Bathroom Tissue. "The article says the museum went down the tubes when its proprietors left town and took their supplies with them."

"Not exactly," Kolb said.

Kolb said that when she moved to Manhattan with the humor weekly in early 2001, she did not take the thousands of rolls of toilet paper with her. Even pre-September 11, that would have elicited some strange looks while traveling. "They wound up in storage in the garage of a friend of my brother's in Elgin," Kolb said.

The odd thing about the new book—which is actually a reissue of a 1997 book with the same title—is that from what I could tell, and I saw the book Monday, there's nothing in it to indicate the museum has left Madison. The article in the *Vancouver Province* says the museum is closed, but nowhere, as far as I could tell, does it say so in the book itself. In fact, in the four pages devoted to the Madison Museum of Bathroom Tissue, people are urged to send in rolls from distant ports: the Pentagon, say, or Alcatraz. The new residents of 305 N. Hamilton might soon find themselves up to their you-know-what in bathroom tissue.

The other odd thing about the book, which does include a number of interesting and weird museums, is that Barry and Patti Levenson's Mount Horeb Mustard Museum isn't mentioned. But then, maybe they won't mind being left out of a volume that celebrates the Cockroach Hall of Fame, run by professional exterminator Michael Bohdan, in Plano, Texas. Bohdan calls himself Cockroach Dundee and has one dead bug he calls "Liberoachi" dressed in sequins and seated at a tiny piano.

A couple of other Wisconsin museums are in the book: the Houdini Historical Center in Appleton and the Hamburger Hall of Fame in Seymour. I must say before Monday I didn't realize Seymour lays claim to the hamburger.

Madison didn't invent toilet paper, but for a brief shining moment we were the center of the TP universe. My guess is that if someone felt like cleaning out a garage in Elgin, we could be again.

═══════════

Monday, January 27, 2003

Hirschfeld Art Finds Home Here

It was a law made to be broken and nowhere was the prohibition of alcohol so joyfully ignored as on the island of Manhattan, where Damon Runyon sat at a small table away from the dance floor in Tex Guinan's speakeasy and collected the stories of guys and dolls he would pass into legend.

In his Runyon biography, Jimmy Breslin noted that Prohibition began in January 1920, and "about a month later, there were more than 15,000 speakeasies" in New York. A speakeasy was a place where you could take in money for selling booze as long as you paid out money in the form of bribes to law enforcement and other authorities. The '20s roared in Manhattan like nowhere else.

There was Babe Ruth and Jimmy Walker and Jimmy Durante and a gangster named Arnold Rothstein, who got himself shot during a poker game in a second-floor hotel room. Rothstein was an associate of another gangster, Champ Segal, who in turn was associated with Ben Siegel, a thug who once did a Hollywood screen test directed by George Raft, an actor famous for portraying gangsters. It was an era of entangling alliances. Champ Segal saw the screen test and said to his friend Ben, "You know how good you were?"

"How good?"

"You'll never have to steal again."

There was also, happily, a young caricaturist named Al Hirschfeld, who found in the speakeasies an oasis from the heavy political discourse young people often engage in. Hirschfeld, who died last week at 99, would become the most famous caricaturist of Broadway show people the world has ever known. But in the 1920s and early '30s—"imbued with a sense of social concern," as his *New York Times* obit put it—Hirschfeld was drawing serious political lithographs for The New Masses. He soon realized those editors cared for art only insofar as it advanced their political agenda. Hirschfeld left politics for Broadway, or as he put it: "I have ever since been closer to Groucho Marx than to Karl."

Meanwhile, there were the speakeasies. How could a developing artist not be interested in a place where the mayor elbowed the police chief out of the way in their mutual rush to spend an illegal dollar? As last week's obituaries mentioned, Hirschfeld's drawings of New York speakeasies were collected in the 1932 book *Manhattan Oases*. The next year Prohibition was repealed. Hirschfeld did the book with his friend, New York newspaperman Gordon Kahn, and along with the drawings came a few paragraphs profiling the speakeasy pictured. The book holds up so well that in June it is being reissued under the title *The Speakeasies of 1932*, with a new introduction by another New York legend, writer Pete Hamill.

What the obituaries did not mention is that the 33 original speakeasy pen-and-ink drawings done by Hirschfeld for the 1932 book are here in Madison, ready for your perusal in the rare books collection of the Wisconsin Historical Society.

This revelation of unburied treasure is getting to be old hat for the society. But who knew? In this case the man who knew to at least ask was Les Fishel, who was director of the society in the early 1960s. On a trip to New York around that time, Fishel met with the artist. "He had a studio in his home in Manhattan," Fishel was saying over the weekend. "He was very friendly, very genial and open. He told me about Nina." Since the birth of his daughter in 1945, Hirschfeld had covertly inserted his daughter's name into all his drawings, often more than once. It was around the time of Fishel's visit that the *New York Times* publisher, Arthur Hays Sulzberger, wrote Hirschfeld asking that the caricaturist let readers know how many "Ninas" to look for in each drawing, which he did.

Fishel could not recall if Hirschfeld promised to send anything to Madison. But in 1961, the original pen-and-inks of *Manhattan Oases* showed up along with a note from Hirschfeld's agent, saying they were a loan from the artist. Two years later another note said the loan had been changed to a gift.

What a gift. Two years ago, the Wisconsin Historical Society loaned six of the drawings to the Museum of the City of New York for a show, "Hirschfeld's New York," which subsequently became a book of the same title. Four of the society's drawings—including the one pictured in today's column, "Barman Ralph"—are included in the book. Today the drawings are all back in Madison.

For Hirschfeld, honors continued to pour in, and in

June, when *Manhattan Oases* is reissued, a theater on Broadway will be named in his honor. That month the artist would have turned 100. "If you live long enough," he said, "everything happens."

Thursday, March 6, 2003

Did UW Discovery Kill Stalin?

On Wednesday, 50 years to the day after the death of Josef Stalin, a Yale professor named Jonathan Brent was considering the circumstances of the Soviet dictator's death.

Wouldn't it be interesting," Brent said, "if one of the biggest rats in history was killed with rat poison?"

Brent's search for the truth of Stalin's final days is recounted in his new book, *Stalin's Last Crime*, co-authored by Russian historian Vladimir Naumov and out next month from HarperCollins.

The authors' search led them to Moscow and some long-buried medical files, and eventually to Madison for discussions with the Wisconsin Alumni Research Foundation.

In a telephone interview Wednesday, Brent said it was a couple of years ago that he and Naumov unearthed the official medical account of Stalin's death, which was given to the Communist Party Central Committee in June 1953.

Stalin had collapsed after a dinner with four top aides, including Nikita Khrushchev, who later headed the Soviet Union. At the time, the cause of Stalin's death was listed as a brain hemorrhage. Brent, however, found records excised from the official report that said Stalin had significant stomach bleeding as well.

Surrounded by Reality

Back in the United States, Brent asked two physicians at Yale, a neurosurgeon and a cardiologist, to study the report. "They both said the same thing," Brent told me. "They said the cause of death was either cerebral hemorrhage or warfarin poisoning."

On Wednesday Brent said, "I didn't know what warfarin was."

One of the doctors explained it is an anticoagulant or "blood thinner" that, in potent doses, is also used as a rat poison that causes vermin to bleed to death. "But I don't know if warfarin had even been invented in 1953," the doctor said.

As Brent soon learned, it had, by UW biochemist Karl Paul Link. Some preliminary research led Brent to contact the Wisconsin Alumni Research Foundation—the "warf" in warfarin—where he was put in touch with emeritus counsel Howard Bremer.

"We get a lot of funny calls but this one was interesting," Bremer told me. Brent was looking for information on warfarin, and Bremer, after a little digging, was able to provide it.

Link had been working in his Madison laboratory one day in 1933 when a farmer from northern Wisconsin appeared carrying a can full of cow's blood. Five of his cows had died mysteriously after eating spoiled sweet clover. Their blood, it turned out, would not coagulate. Link studied it and, over the next decade, developed warfarin, which by the late 1940s was being marketed worldwide and was pumping millions into WARF.

Years later Link's widow, Elizabeth Link, donated the family home in the Highlands to be used to promote world peace issues. Retired Madison fire chief Ed Durkin became director of the Link Friendship House and proved a tireless advocate for lessening tensions between the United States and the Soviet Union. In 1992, he hosted at the Link house the Soviet cosmonaut Sergei Krikalev, who became the first

Russian ever invited on a U.S. space shuttle as well one of the first three residents of the International Space Station.

If the Link house has done much for the cause of world peace, there is wonderful symmetry in the likelihood that the drug that started it all, warfarin, may have been employed a half century earlier in Moscow to rid the Russians of the dictator who Brent said was seriously considering a nuclear strike on the United States.

Whether it was a brain hemorrhage or poison that killed Stalin may never be definitively known, but the records uncovered by Brent and Naumov point to warfarin. Stalin's top lieutenants were known to be terrified of him. And not only did the dictator have stomach bleeding, there is also evidence that Stalin was ill at least a full day before he suffered a stroke.

"I hope the book causes a clamoring for an autopsy," Brent said, adding that he has found another doctor, at Wayne State University, who says that with a sample of Stalin's tissue he could say conclusively if warfarin was used. Other physicians are less certain an autopsy would prove definitive.

Stalin was 73 when he died in 1953. Two years later, the U.S. president, Dwight D. Eisenhower, suffered a heart attack but survived with the aid of a blood thinner. His doctors prescribed warfarin.

Saturday, September 20, 2003

Recalling One Colorful Character

When my choice for colorful character of the past century in Madison, Marion Roberts, died quietly in Texas in 1977, it was the first quiet event of his life.

Earlier this week Brennan Nardi, managing editor of *Madison* magazine, was talking about the magazine's plans to feature, in an upcoming issue, "where are they now" updates on some 125 Madisonians of note featured in the magazine over the years. It should be a fun read, but it's a terrible pain to research. I know, because in 1992, when I was editing the magazine, we did the same kind of feature with the 50 Madisonians featured in photographer Doug Edmunds' locally famous 1980 "Citizen" poster. After 12 years it wasn't like trying to find Leo Burt, but it was close.

Marion Roberts never made any of those lists. He came and went like a comet. But he is my colorful character of the last century in this city and, who knows, maybe the next. Who would you nominate today? There is nobody.

So we are left with Roberts. In the fall of 1993, I was sitting in Madison's most venerable steakhouse, Smoky's, on University Avenue. The proprietor, Leonard Schmock, whose nickname adorns the restaurant, was still alive, and had agreed to talk to me about Marion Roberts. He sat at a table near the bar and growled at the employees getting ready to open.

"Nobody had more fun than Marion Roberts," Schmock said. "I've never seen anyone like him, before or since."

"What kind of things did he do?"

"One time he was flying to South America to check out an underwater gold mine," Schmock said. "He asked me to come along."

They landed in Colombia. "You know the first thing you do in Colombia?" Schmock said. "You get a gun. Then you get the permits to mine. Then you start a party that lasts four days." Eventually Roberts and Schmock rented a barge and went looking for the mine. "But some bandits started shooting at us."

"What did you do?"

The Best of Doug Moe on Madison

"We pulled out."

Roberts first came to Madison in 1959. He loved to talk and throw money at bartenders, and he was always being paged at Rohde's, a downtown steakhouse that hopped in those days. Roberts grew quiet only on the subject of his past. Few here knew that a year before he arrived in Madison, Roberts was indicted by a Texas grand jury on three counts of theft by false pretense. He was a con man.

When he came here, though, he was a con man with a big budget. He'd charter planes and fly friends to New York City on a whim. Walter Winchell wrote in his New York gossip column: "The Copa's biggest spender in years is an industrialist named Roberts from Madison, Wisconsin."

Eventually some Madisonians got taken, but for a long time the vast amounts of cash Roberts burned through came from a line of credit on a bank in Oklahoma. His cover here in Madison was the development of Foamalum, a foamed aluminum substance light enough to float on water but heavy enough to use in building. There was a plant on Fish Hatchery Road that would manufacture it, and NASA was said to want Foamalum for a re-entry shield. It sounded too good to be true and it was.

What was true was that Roberts knew a lot of celebrities, especially from sports. He brought Mickey Mantle to Madison to address a service club. He produced Rocky Marciano to serve as king of the George Holmes Rodeo, and, off stage, Marciano whispered to Schmock, "I'd rather fight Joe Louis than get on a horse."

The beginning of the end for Roberts came when he persuaded state senator Reuben LaFave to "introduce" a 19-year-old singer, Lisa Marne, in the state senate chamber. It was July 1965 and Roberts' interest in Miss Marne extended beyond her voice. On being introduced, Marne grabbed the mike and launched into "Call Me Irresponsible." The senators squirmed but she had the bit in her teeth and wound up doing three numbers, which did a number on Roberts.

Reporters wanted to know more about the guy who could get his girlfriend a singing gig in the state capitol.

Roberts wound up serving nine months in federal prison on tax evasion charges. He survived that but couldn't survive having the cash faucet in Oklahoma turned off. Ill with cancer, Roberts went home to El Paso to die. He was 52.

"You might say the roof caved in," Schmock told me. "His account was chopped off. I got a letter saying don't send any more bills to Enid, Oklahoma."

Schmock grinned at the memory. "I probably spent some money I wouldn't have spent if I hadn't known him. But I also wouldn't have all the memories of the great times we had."

≡≡≡

Wednesday, September 24, 2003

Ugliest Couch and Proud of It

Camille Hempel, who has the ugliest couch in America and $5,000 to prove it, first went soft on sofas while living just off West Mifflin Street in 1990.

The area, known to those of a certain vintage as Miffland, is ground zero for sagging sofas. No student housing porch is complete without one. The couch should have coffee stains, a spring sticking out, and when you look under the lumpy cushions it's like cutting open the shark's belly in *Jaws*.

Hempel, who grew up in Janesville and now lives in Brooklyn, New York, was in her last year at UW–Madison in 1990 when she decided that it was finally time for her apartment couch to go to the big living room in the sky. Her boyfriend's cat had pretty well shredded it. Somewhat reluctantly, she dragged the couch to the curb.

"An hour later, it was on the porch across the street," Hempel was saying Monday. "I got kind of jealous. I had to look at it every time I went out the front door."

Hempel wound up taking a picture of the couch, and with that began an odyssey that culminated last week when the studio audience at Tuesday's *Live With Regis and Kelly* show in New York City picked Hempel's current couch—pink and brown, with its right side supported by a cinder block— as the ugliest couch in the United States.

The contest, sponsored by the Sure Fit slipcover company, drew more than 1,000 entries. First prize was $5,000. Online voting—more than 50,000 ballots were cast—narrowed the field to three, and last week all three couches and their owners were chatted up by Regis Philbin on national TV. When the audience's votes were totaled, the 35-year-old Hempel emerged victorious.

"I'm on couch cloud nine," she told me.

Hempel is a deserving winner. It's almost certain nobody in the United States has spent more time considering couches than Hempel. She has photographed them, painted them—her UW degree is in art—and rescued them from untold numbers of curbs. "I have hundreds of pictures of couches," Hempel said. "I got obsessed with the whole thing."

She moved to New York in 1992; her sister, Heather Hempel, still lives in Madison. In New York City, Hempel, who earns a modest living designing and making jewelry— "I'm basically a starving artist," she said—encountered a whole new world of decaying masterpieces.

"I'll see them on the curbs when I'm riding my bike around the city and then come back later at night," Hempel said. Sometimes it's just to take a photo. "I have a red El Camino and I'll shine the lights on the couch," she said.

"Those photos can look like a crime scene."

Other times, she takes the whole couch. That was the case four years ago when a friend called to report a brown and pink sofa sitting curbside in Queens. Hempel took the couch home to Brooklyn and had to immediately stare down a revolt from her roommates. Some people look at an ugly couch and see, well, an ugly couch.

Hempel pleaded the sofa's case and won a stay of execution. A good thing, too, because in August, when another friend was shopping online for slip covers and came across the Sure Fit Ugly Couch Contest, Hempel knew she had a contender.

"I set up my camera in my living room, which is also my kitchen," Hempel said. She snapped the photo and sent it off to the contest, where the competition turned out to be heated.

"We used to ask people to include themselves in the picture of the sofa," a Sure Fit executive, Maris F. Thalberg, recently told the *New York Times*. "But some people sent pictures of themselves naked."

The *Times* actually had someone reporting backstage from the *Regis and Kelly* show last week. Besides Hempel and her cinder block special, the two other finalists were a velvet red sofa from Virginia and what the *Times* called "a plaid monstrosity" from Iowa. Those couch owners were flown in at the show's expense and put up at a classy Manhattan hotel. Since Hempel lives in Brooklyn, the producers hadn't thought that she, too, might enjoy such pampering.

"When do I ever get to stay in a fancy hotel in Manhattan?" Hempel asked. The producers gave her tickets to a Broadway show instead.

On the day of the show, the *Times* reporter caught up with Hempel backstage just before air time. "I'm totally in it for the glory," she said.

Now the glory is hers. First the live telecast of her

victory, then the *Times* article. This week Hempel was wondering where it all might end when a representative of a prestigious publisher of art books got in touch to wonder if there wasn't maybe a book in all those photographs of all those couches.

"We have a meeting set for next week," Camille Hempel said.

As of the spring of 2005, Camille did not have a couch book deal, but she wrote to tell me that she had acquired a tattoo—of an ugly couch, of course.

═══════════

Monday, October 27, 2003

Terror Cell on Fordem Avenue?

In a concrete room in Pennsylvania last week, a man from Yemen named Ashraf Al-Jailani, whom the U.S. government says is an international terrorist, heard a portion of the case against him.

During the proceeding, an Akron, Ohio, FBI agent, Roger Charnesky, testified that one of the most compelling pieces of evidence against Al-Jailani, who denies he is a terrorist of any kind, is a Wisconsin identification card that showed Al-Jailani with a Madison address.

A second terrorism suspect had the same Madison address, Charnesky testified. This second man was identified only as Suspect B. Information on both the men was discovered when the FBI searched the Chicago home of a third man, identified as Mr. Khaleel, whom the feds say bought computers and satellite equipment for al-Qaida out of the house in Chicago.

If this sounds wild now, we're just getting started.

It's a story that begins not with terrorism but with domestic abuse. In 1994, Ashraf Al-Jailani was studying in Japan at Shimane University when he met a young American named Michelle Swensen, a zoology student at Kent State in Ohio, who had won a scholarship to spend a year studying in Japan. The two eventually married and moved to Kent, Ohio, near Akron.

In December 1998, the couple had been shopping at a mall when they got into an argument in the parking lot and Michelle's glasses were knocked from her face. She ran back into the mall, found a cop, and—inadvertently, she later said—started a process that culminated in a deportation order for her husband. The 1996 Immigration Act makes a domestic violence conviction automatic grounds for deportation.

The couple, who now have three young children, fought the order, and a prominent columnist, Anthony Lewis of the *New York Times*, visited Kent and wrote about the case, saying the "harshness" of the Immigration Act would "destroy" the family. On January 9, 2001, Ohio Governor Bob Taft pardoned Al-Jailani on the misdemeanor charge, meaning he could stay in the United States.

In the meantime, Al-Jailani, with a background in chemistry, had taken a job with Akron-based GOJO Industries, maker of skin care products; he worked in quality assurance.

All appeared normal until a year ago, October 23, 2002, when immigration agents arrested Al-Jailani at work while the FBI searched his home. Though never charged, Al-Jailani was taken to the Berks County Prison near Reading, Pennsylvania.

In March of this year, a Pennsylvania immigration judge, Walt Durling, ordered Al-Jailani—still not charged with anything—released on bond, saying he posed no flight risk or risk to the community. Durling issued his ruling in the morning, and by afternoon the Department of Homeland Security had blocked it.

In July, Homeland Security asked Durling to vacate his order and have Al-Jailani held without bond. Durling said he'd need to see evidence of why he should do that. Last week was the bond hearing, in York, Pennsylvania.

Cleveland Plain Dealer reporter Karen R. Long covered the hearing and described the government's main witness, FBI Special Agent Roger Charnesky, "glistening with perspiration," offering this assessment of the imprisoned Al-Jailani: An al-Qaida "first-stringer, highly educated, highly trained, and highly motivated." The agent said further that Al-Jailani's employer, GOJO Industries, with abundant explosive and flammable chemicals on premises, was the probable target.

According to the *Plain Dealer*, Charnesky testified that U.S. Attorney General John Ashcroft had declassified some intelligence for last week's hearing. The Madison references appear in this new evidence. In April 1999, while searching the Chicago home of suspected al-Qaida operative "Mr. Khaleel," FBI agents discovered Al-Jailani's Ohio business card, along with an identification card for another terrorism suspect—Suspect B—that listed 1826 "Fordham Ave." in Madison as Suspect B's address. Three years later—last October—when the FBI searched Al-Jailani's home, they found a Wisconsin identification card in his name with the same "Fordham Avenue" address.

The matching addresses, along with phone records indicating Al-Jailani made calls to a New York number linked to terrorists, make the likelihood Al-Jailani is a terrorist "a mathematical probability," Charnesky testified.

A number of questions come to mind (apart from the evidence as reported seeming a bit thin), including whether anyone realizes Fordem Avenue is spelled incorrectly. Questions like: Do the authorities believe Al-Jailani and

Suspect B actually lived in an apartment in Madison? Or did they just use the address on some identification cards? Is Suspect B still at large, and what is he suspected of?

Unfortunately, when Mary Trotman, the FBI's supervisory senior resident agent in Akron, returned my phone call Friday afternoon, she said she couldn't talk about the case.

Too bad. If you go to court in Pennsylvania with a terrorism suspect from Ohio and say the key evidence is their shared address in Madison, it follows that Madison residents might be curious. The bond hearing continues this week.

═══

Tuesday, October 28, 2003

Yes, Terror Suspect Lived Here

Ashraf Al-Jailani, the Yemen-born Ohio man who has been held for a year by the U.S. government—without being charged—on suspicion of being an international terrorist, did indeed live in Madison for a short time in 1996, in the same apartment building of a second man believed to be a terrorist with links to al-Qaida.

The shared Madison address on Fordem Avenue was said by the FBI at a hearing last week in Pennsylvania to be a key piece of the government's case against Al-Jailani.

I wrote about the case Monday. At the time I couldn't be sure whether Al-Jailani had lived here, or only had a Wisconsin ID with a Madison address. The ID was introduced as evidence against him at the hearing.

On Monday, Al-Jailani's attorney, Farhad Sethna of

Akron, Ohio, told me his understanding is that Al-Jailani came to Madison on first arriving in the United States in 1996. Al-Jailani had met an American woman he eventually married, Michele Swensen of Ohio, in college in Japan in 1994.

Al-Jailani came to Madison because he had a friend here who owned a gas station, and Al-Jailani worked there to raise some money before joining Swensen in Ohio. That, at least, appears to be Al-Jailani's story.

The government—the Akron FBI refused to discuss the case with me last week—believes that Al-Jailani was in Madison to discuss terror tactics with a second man, identified in court in Pennsylvania only as "Suspect B." This second man shared the Fordem address with Al-Jailani, though they lived in separate apartments.

The hearing last week in Pennsylvania took place because a judge, Walt Durling, had told the government he was going to set bail for Al-Jailani unless the government presented evidence of why he should not. Durling had wanted to set bail back in March but was blocked by the Department of Homeland Security.

Akron FBI agent Roger Charnesky testified last week, under tight security in a concrete block room in York, Pennsylvania, that Al-Jailani is an al-Qaida "first-stringer, highly educated, highly trained, and highly motivated."

Charnesky said U.S. Attorney General John Ashcroft had ordered some of the evidence against Al-Jailani declassified for Wednesday's hearing.

Al-Jailani has consistently denied the charges. He'd earlier had trouble with federal immigration authorities because of allegations of domestic abuse toward Swensen.

While last week the government presented some other evidence against Al-Jailani—including phone records showing calls from his home in Ohio to New York numbers with al-Qaida links—his connection with Suspect B in Madison was crucial to the government's case.

Surrounded by Reality

At the hearing, Sethna, Al-Jailani's defense lawyer, asked Charnesky if he could provide any more information on the mysterious Suspect B who allegedly drew Al-Jailani to Madison.

"That's classified," Charnesky replied.

It would be nice to know, for instance, if Suspect B is still at large, or still living on Fordem Avenue, for that matter. Doubtful, but the government isn't saying.

What did come out of the hearing in Pennsylvania last week was that it all started in April 1999, when the FBI searched the Chicago home of a man identified only as "Mr. Kahleel," who was linked to al-Qaida. In the house, agents found Al-Jailani's Ohio business card, as well as contact information for Suspect B—the contact information was the Fordem Avenue address.

Three years later, when Al-Jailani was arrested in Ohio and his house was searched, a Wisconsin ID with the same Fordem Avenue address was discovered in Al-Jailani's fanny pack. It took the FBI several months to realize that the Fordem Avenue address was the same as Suspect B's.

When he was arrested a year ago, Al-Jailani, who has a chemistry background, was working for GOJO Industries in Akron, a manufacturer of skin care products, in quality control. Charnesky, the FBI agent, testified that the company's highly flammable inventory was the likely terrorist target. A company spokeswoman told the *Akron Beacon Journal* Friday that Al-Jailani did not work near where the chemicals are mixed.

Al-Jailani's lawyer, Sethna—who is working pro bono—said Monday the hearing is set to continue Friday.

===

Wednesday, November 5, 2003

War at Home Goes on DVD

This was 25 years ago in an editing studio in New York City. A couple of kid filmmakers, Glenn Silber and Barry Alexander Brown, had spent the last several years sifting through old TV news reports from Madison stations.

When they weren't doing that, they were on the street with their hands out looking for money. No one thought they would finish the film. By this point, Silber and Brown were getting along so well they barely spoke to each other.

But they'd put together a negative, more than three hours long, and they asked a few trusted friends who were in the area for an independent film festival to take a look. They loved it. "And when you get it down under two hours," one said, "I'll be happy to look at it again."

Silber and Brown looked at each other.

"I had known there was something wrong with it," Silber was saying Tuesday. "But Barry and I weren't getting along, and we were one day from sending it out. One day. But that comment broke our logjam and we got to work cutting it."

The finished result, *The War at Home*—which tells the story of Madison during the Vietnam War years—was eventually nominated for an Academy Award. It is one of the most important and enduring portraits of this city in the last century, and Silber was talking about it this week because next month, *The War at Home* will be available on DVD for the first time.

Unfortunately, there are no additional director

commentaries or other add-ons for the DVD. That other hour of footage isn't around, either, except in bits and pieces at the Wisconsin Historical Society. But while the movie has been available on VHS for some time, Silber is pleased that the high-resolution DVD is coming out, and thinks it will introduce the film to a new generation of viewers.

"With young people," Silber said, "talking to them about Vietnam is like telling them about World War I."

With the publication of David Maraniss' *They Marched Into Sunlight* and now the re-release of *The War at Home*, this is definitely the season of Madison and the Vietnam War. People who have read *Sunlight* should be interested in seeing actual news footage of the Dow Chemical demonstrations. That footage became available while Silber and Brown were researching the film.

Today Silber is a producer for ABC News' *20/20* newsmagazine in New York. Brown is best known as editor for a number of Spike Lee movies, including *Summer of Sam* and *Malcolm X*.

In their Madison days, Silber and Brown were broke but accomplished. Before *The War at Home* they had produced a documentary on Joe McCarthy for Wisconsin Public Television. Silber had been thinking about a piece on the Madison war protests even before the McCarthy film. At one point, around 1975, he mentioned it to George Talbot at the Wisconsin Historical Society. Talbot was responsible for the film and video archive and he told Silber, "You might get lucky."

What Talbot knew was that a Madison TV newsman, Blake Kellogg, who had watched the nightsticks fly on Bascom Hill and reported it all to viewers of Channel 27, wanted to get that archival news footage away from the mice in the WKOW-TV basement. Kellogg knew the value of what he had and arranged for the station to donate it to the Historical Society. In a deal sealed only by a handshake, Brown and Silber agreed to view and catalog all that film if they could use the pertinent parts in their film at no charge. Brown watched most of it while Silber was out hustling money to complete the film. The footage is riveting. It includes a 1963 demonstration against the U.S. presence in Vietnam that drew 300—Paul Soglin among them—in front of the Memorial Union. "That may have been the first campus demonstration against the war anywhere," Silber said, "and it's on film."

Silber said one of his regrets is that a verbal confrontation between state Senator Gordon Roseleip, R-Darlington, and embattled UW–Madison Chancellor William Sewell wound up out of the trimmed version of the film. "There wasn't a gap between their points of view," Silber said. "There was an abyss."

Still, that abyss is apparent in the finished movie. It remains a vivid reminder of an incredible era, even as we are always reminded that time marches on. This week, Glenn Silber will be back in Madison, without regard to the war at home. His daughter is thinking about college, and she wants to see Wisconsin.

===

Tuesday, November 25, 2003

A Slice of Life from the "Pieman"

Joel Skornicka, the former Madison mayor who has returned to town full time as a consultant, was lunching Friday at the Avenue, which led some diners at the next table to recall the time that Skornicka got hit by a Boston cream pie moments before being sworn in as mayor.

Surrounded by Reality

Jeff Scott Olson, the local civil rights attorney, had been doing some research last week on Weedstock when he came across a news account of the pie thrower being brought to justice 14 years after hurling the pie. Olson mentioned it at lunch, and that in turn led me to do some research over the weekend, which brought the startling discovery that Skornicka was not pied by a run-of-the-mill flake. The *State Journal*'s report at the time identified the pie thrower only as "a New York native who has 'pied' several local politicians in recent years."

In fact, the pie thrower was already nationally famous, or rather infamous.

Aron Kay, the guy who nailed Skornicka, has gone down in history as the founder of a movement. In 2000, when Canada was enduring a rash of pie throwing at elected officials, the *Calgary Herald* noted: "Pie-tossing became a feature of North American politics when Yippie Aron Kay, the 'Great American Pieman,' took up cream pies as part of his group's anti-establishment crusade."

Kay's Madison moment came on April 17, 1979. The 29-year-old Kay approached Skornicka in the City-County Building and hit him with the pie. Kay then tried to flee, but Paul Soglin, the outgoing mayor who witnessed the assault, cornered Kay until a police detective, George Croal, arrived and placed Kay under arrest.

Soglin, who had been pied himself while in office, was furious. Skornicka pretty much laughed it off, saying, "I did not intend to start my lunch so early."

Charged with disorderly conduct, Kay didn't show at his Dane County court appearance. Another arrest warrant was issued and was outstanding for 14 years, until May 31, 1993, when an Arena police officer named Curt Wilkinson stopped to question a hitchhiker on Highway 14. It turned out to be Kay, in the area visiting relatives. A background search revealed he was wanted in Madison.

"I thought the statute of limitations had run out," Kay

said.

It had not. Kay was transported to the Dane County Jail, got bailed out, and in June entered a not guilty plea. That was the last of the news accounts.

I called the County Clerk's office Monday and asked if they could track down what happened to him. This is what happened: Kay changed his plea to no contest and in September 1993 paid a $275 fine.

By that time, Kay had thrown his last pie. He retired in 1992, after catching anti-abortion advocate Randall Terry with a custard pie.

Before retiring, though, Kay had racked up a veritable who's who of targets. Over the years he pied physicist Edward Teller, the father of the A-bomb; former CIA Director William Colby; conservative columnist William F. Buckley; LBJ adviser McGeorge Bundy; ERA opponent Phyllis Schafly; the artist Andy Warhol; and Watergate figure E. Howard Hunt.

Nowadays, whenever someone catches a pie in the face, a reporter in the area is likely to track down Kay. The *San Francisco Examiner* ran a lengthy profile of Kay when Mayor Willie Brown was pied in 1998, and the *Chicago Daily Herald* did likewise when Illinois Governor George Ryan caught one in 2000.

Both papers reported he was living in New York City. Naturally, Kay has his own website, www.pieman.org, which is filled with rants against George W. Bush and in favor of marijuana. He told the *Daily Herald* that he retired from pie throwing because of "a health problem."

None of the many stories I found about Kay mentioned his having pied Joel Skornicka in Madison. And none of the Madison stories at the time said why he picked Skornicka, who was fairly liberal and not in the pattern of Kay's conservative targets.

I reached Kay, now 54, in Brooklyn, New York, Monday night.

"Aron, why did you do it?"

"*TakeOver* flew me out to pie him," Kay said, referring to the Madison underground paper of that era. "I crossed state lines to throw a pie."

He said he understood *TakeOver*'s motives in hiring him to be that they were upset Skornicka had been elected Madison mayor in a tight race over Jim Rowen, a candidate they perceived to be more progressive on tenants' rights.

Kay confirmed that he is retired from pie throwing. "Though I am available for consultation," he said.

He said that of late he has been networking with an eye toward next summer's Republican National Convention in New York City. He didn't say whether he might come out of retirement with a pie. Maybe he'll just poke around the trash bins outside the convention, a sideline he began as a way of gaining information about the same time he started throwing pies.

"I stole Richard Nixon's garbage in 1980," Kay said.

═══════

Wednesday, December 10, 2003

Nick's Bump: Hear It, Drink It

This is a story of music and travel and a drink that might, as a friend of mine used to say, set you free.

It begins two decades ago in the near west side home of Ralph and Carol Andreano. The Andreanos are music lovers, and the jazz and classical sounds in the house made an impression on their son, who would later become famous in Madison and beyond as a disc jockey named Nick Nice.

"My dad traveled around the world," Nick said in a

2000 interview with Al Richie. Ralph Andreano, of course, is a health economist of international renown. "Every time he'd travel," Nick said, "he'd always bring back a couple tapes from each country, and so I'd always get exposed to different cultures."

On Tuesday, Nick said: "He'd do that, and we also lived in Switzerland for a time and traveled around Europe. The music was a big part of my life growing up."

Nick built a vast and eclectic record collection, and then, while studying abroad in Paris, he saw a DJ in a small club who used smoke and lights and a charismatic presence to turn disc jockeying into performance art. Nick came back to Madison and began a famous run doing just that at the Cardinal Bar.

Jump forward a decade. It is 2001, and Nick is spinning records at the Opus Lounge, a hot new bar on King Street in the shadow of the state capitol.

"He'd need a little pick-me-up," Opus manager Ethan Lund said Tuesday.

"I'd have worked Friday and Saturday night, and by the time Sunday rolled around I was pretty tired," Nick said. "I'd ask for a coffee or espresso, and of course the bartenders wouldn't go for that. They started experimenting, putting different things in."

The bartenders, with feedback from Nick, arrived at a daunting concoction that included Stolichnaya vanilla vodka, with smaller amounts of several liqueurs: Frangelico, Bailey's, and Godiva white and dark. A shot of espresso completed the recipe.

"People would see them making it," Nick said, "and ask to try it. Or they would come in during the week and ask for that thing that Nick drinks.'"

Eventually it went on the drink menu at the Opus as *Nick's Bump.* "I understand that for a time it was the most popular drink at the Opus," Nick said. "Much to the chagrin of the bartenders. It is a pain to make."

Surrounded by Reality

One Opus customer who not long ago tried it and liked it was Ben Sidran, the Madison jazz legend. At the time Sidran was in the studio recording a new album, which will be released next month. Sidran's admiration for the drink was such that he decided to name his new record after it. That's a refreshing notion in these temperate times. I doubt *Nick's Bump* is on the Atkins diet, but so what? As the novelist Jim Harrison pointed out recently, the possibility exists that life should be more than a long self-improvement course.

It was actually Ben's sax player, Bob Rockwell, who had written a song that needed a name and saw *Nick's Bump* on the Opus menu. "I liked the name because it had a 1960s feel, and that was what we were after on this record," Sidran said.

Unknown to Sidran at the time, there were a few connections to make his naming of the CD almost eerily appropriate. For one thing, the Sidran home is near the Andreano home on the near west side. For another, on those distant Sunday nights when Nick Nice needed a pick-me-up before spinning his records at the Opus, his music of choice was the very kind of 1960s groove instrumental jazz that Sidran was laying down in the tracks that became *Nick's Bump*.

"Those Sunday nights were for listening, not dancing," Nick said.

The CD has already been released in Europe to much acclaim, and Ben, along with a band that included his son, Leo Sidran, just got back from a successful tour that included stops in France, Spain, and Italy.

In the course of the tour the musicians would occasionally find themselves thirsty, and given the new CD the tour was in part to promote, there would come a time when someone thought to order a Nick's Bump. In Paris and Madrid the request brought puzzled frowns, but with a little coaching a serviceable version was produced. "By the time

we left Milan they said it was going on the menu of the Blue
Note," Sidran said, referring to the club they played
December 1–6.

Technology allows the new CD, out here in January, to
include an interview with Nick Nice about the origins of the
drink. Plug the CD into your computer, and Nick starts
talking about the Opus Lounge. That's where Ben Sidran
headed the other day when his plane back from Europe
touched down in Madison. He ordered a Nick's Bump and
had nothing to explain.

═══════════

Monday, December 29, 2003

Recalling the Great Daydreamer

Of all the people who "got away" in 2003, the one I most
wish I had known was George Plimpton, the writer, editor,
and bon vivant who died in his sleep at 76 in New York City
in late September.

Plimpton made it to Madison a few times, and it is
altogether fitting that at least one of his visits happened by
mistake. Plimpton, after all, was a connoisseur of the offbeat.
What happened to him here in November 1974 was
certainly strange, and I have not seen it related since his
death.

Plimpton was scheduled to speak at Marquette
University, and his plane from New York landed at Mitchell
Field late on the afternoon of his speech. Unfortunately,
when the plane took off on the final leg of its flight to
Madison, Plimpton was still aboard.

On landing at the Dane County airport, Plimpton

deplaned and went to a rental car desk in the airport.

"Can you give me directions to Marquette University?"

"In Milwaukee?" the clerk asked.

"Why, of course," Plimpton said.

At some point it dawned on Plimpton that he was a bit farther from Marquette than anticipated. "It was all very confusing," the desk clerk later told the Associated Press.

But Plimpton duly rented his car, and the AP report continued: "Plimpton was soon on the road to Milwaukee, and Marquette officials persuaded the sheriff's office to have a motor escort waiting at the county line to provide him with guidance to the school."

That took a lot of doing, from a logistical standpoint, but fate was not yet done with the author, as the AP noted: "Plimpton drove past the waiting escort."

Still, there was a happy ending: "He found his way to the downtown university alone, arriving only 15 minutes behind schedule."

What I like most about the story is that when Plimpton finally gave his speech that night at Marquette, he never mentioned his airplane adventure. Why would he? As the AP observed, he had "missed his target in Plimptonian style." Getting off at the wrong airport and driving past a waiting police escort was just another day in the life of a writer who always zeroed in on what was eccentric, bizarre, outrageous, or at least humorous in American life.

He specialized in Walter Mitty-like forays into personal journalism, playing quarterback for the Detroit Lions, percussion for the New York Philharmonic, and so on, and then writing about it in books like *Paper Lion* and *Out of Their League.* He was friends with the famous—Ernest Hemingway, the Kennedy family, Warren Beatty, and dozens of others.

But my favorite Plimpton pieces were when he found an ordinary individual engaged in an extraordinary activity, and none was better than the June 1998 piece Plimpton wrote about Larry Walters, a 33-year-old California truck driver who in July 1982 tied 42 helium-filled balloons to a lawn chair and launched himself into the skies over Southern California.

Things went wrong almost from the start. He had used a rope to tether himself to a friend's 1962 Chevrolet so he'd hover perhaps 100 feet above the ground. But the tether broke, and then, when Walters reached 15,000 feet, a gust of wind caused him to drop the gun he planned to use to puncture the balloons and accomplish his descent. A moment later, a commercial airliner passing nearby radioed the Los Angeles airport: "This is TWA 231, level at 16,000 feet. We have a man in a chair attached to balloons in our 10 o'clock position, range five miles."

The helium eventually leaked from the balloons, and Walters got down safely. Plimpton interviewed him a short time later, but then Walters called and asked him not to write the story. It says a lot for Plimpton that he agreed—what a wonderfully zany story to have to spike!—but when he did write it, 15 years later, it was all the better, and certainly more poignant, because it was after Walters put a gun to his head while hiking in the San Gabriel Mountains.

Plimpton's last visit to Madison—at least I think it was his last—was in February 1987 when he came to address a state tourism conference. He got off at the right airport that time, and his speech might have served as a summation of his life. He said if he'd learned anything over the years it was that almost all people yearn to experience "the great daydreams" in life.

He then told his Madison audience of his own first experience with a great daydream. He was in college and trying to break into the *Harvard Lampoon* when an editor suggested running in the Boston Marathon and writing about it.

"They did not specify that I had to run the race from the beginning," Plimpton said. Instead, he said, he entered the 26-mile marathon "about a block and a half from the finish—and I entered it immediately behind the fellow who was leading the race. He looked over his shoulder and there I was, fresh as a daisy. This poor man put on a desperate sprint, which is quite a feat if you've run 26 miles, and he managed to cross the finish line before I did, which gives you some sense of my speed."

The *Capital Times* headline after that speech read: "Plimpton just wants to do the impossible." He had a great time trying.

2004

Thursday, January 29, 2004

Hirsch Wore Greatness with Grace

This was 1991, at a restaurant in Miami. The annual meeting of the NFL Alumni Association was in town, and wherever you went celebrities were being elbowed out of the way by legends.

At an unobtrusive table in the restaurant sat Elroy Hirsch, in Miami with some Madison friends. Many people stopped by the table to say hello to Elroy, and at one point a young man asked to shake hands.

"Mr. Hirsch," he said, "I just had to shake your hand. I've watched you on film, and you were the greatest."

When the man left, Elroy turned to Madison area banker Jan Hogan and said, "Who was that?"

"Legs," Hogan said, using a diminutive of Hirsch's "Crazylegs" nickname, "that was Barry Sanders."

In a room full of football greats, Elroy Hirsch, who died here Wednesday at 80, stood out. He set numerous records, but it was more than that. Charisma? Maybe.

Surrounded by Reality

Whatever it was, when Jim Murray, probably the greatest sportswriter who ever lived, lost the sight in his remaining good eye in 1979, he wrote a column saying one thing he'd like to see again was "Elroy Hirsch going for a long one from Bob Waterfield."

Hirsch was teamed with Waterfield on the Los Angeles Rams, where he played pro football after first making his name in the Midwest. A native of Wausau, he played college football with both the Badgers and Michigan. But it was when Hirsch returned to Madison, as athletic director in the late 1960s—after a disastrous decade for UW athletics—that he cemented his legend here.

It could not have been an easy decision to come back. Elroy had settled into an executive's job with the Rams. He had a clothing contract from a company named after Catalina Island. He was surrounded by sun, surf, and admirers, and he walked away from it all to become athletic director at a school that didn't seem sure it even wanted athletics.

When Elroy arrived in Madison for his second act, the football team couldn't win a game. There was debt and deferred maintenance on facilities.

By the time Hirsch retired two decades later, UW athletics had turned around. Elroy's tenure did not have the corporate polish we see out of Camp Randall today, and there were some mistakes in judgment over the years. Taken as a whole, however, his success was large—and it's doubtful any athletic director anywhere ever had more fun. At away football games, Elroy's hotel door was always open. When Butch Strickler arrived with cheese and sausage, the beer was already on ice and buddies like Jerry Hill and Wayne Esser were telling stories. It was a floating bologna bash that lasted 20 years.

If it seemed like Elroy was always "on," it's because that is how you most often saw him, in public, sheathed in glamour like a movie star. There were quiet times, too, with his beloved wife, Ruth. In later years, when Elroy's health was up and down, they'd go to dinner at Chi-Chi's restaurant on the west side, not far from their condo.

I remember seeing the two of them there one night in 1999, sitting at a small corner table. I went up to say hello, and on their way out, they stopped by our table. I was able to tell my son, "You just shook hands with one of the greatest football players who ever lived."

Our waitress, who had been listening, said, "And two of the nicest people you will ever meet."

I last spoke to Ruth in late summer, when a UW alum, Milwaukee attorney Peter Christianson, had asked about the movie of Elroy's life story, *Crazylegs*, filmed in 1953 and starring Hirsch as himself. "You know, Elroy hadn't even acted in a high school play," Ruth said with a laugh. Still, he did a good job as himself, and Christianson—noting that the film was not available on video or DVD—wondered if there were any prints at all. Ruth said she and the couple's two children each had a print.

Ruth said she'd loan us the movie if we wanted to arrange a showing on campus (something Christianson had suggested), but it never quite came together. Maybe next year. It would be great to hear the crowd reaction when Elroy tells his dad, who wants him to work in the family hardware store, that he wants nothing more than to play football for Wisconsin.

I'm thinking now about what Jim Murray wrote, in that column about losing his eyesight, and his desire to see Elroy Hirsch catch just one more pass. "Come to think of it," Murray wrote, "I'm lucky." After all, he had his memories. When it comes to Elroy Hirsch, we all do.

Saturday, January 31, 2004

How Elroy Came to Be "Crazylegs"

Around the world this week, the death of Elroy Hirsch was headline news. In virtually all the stories, the origin of his famous Crazylegs nickname was explained.

In a short story on its front page Thursday, the *Wisconsin State Journal* noted: "Elroy Hirsch was given his nickname by *Chicago Daily News* sportswriter Francis Powers. Covering the Badgers' 13-7 victory over Great Lakes Naval Station October 17, 1942, at Soldier Field in Chicago, Powers wrote, 'Hirsch ran like a demented duck. His crazy legs were gyrating in six different directions all at the same time during a 61-yard touchdown run that cemented the win.' From that day forward, Hirsch was 'Crazylegs.'"

A similar explanation ran in most papers. Then on Thursday night, I got the following note from a reader named Ed Daub, who said he thought the Crazylegs nickname was bestowed on Hirsch one game earlier, when the Badgers played Missouri on October 10, 1942, at Camp Randall Stadium.

"I was a freshman and a cheerleader in 1942," Daub wrote. "In those days we were allowed to stand on the sidelines, and I distinctly remember Elroy hurdling over a tackler in the game against Missouri, a game that ended in a 10-10 tie and yet brought prestige to UW because Missouri was highly rated. I always thought that it was his hurdling with legs splayed out that marked the birth of the nickname Crazylegs."

Mr. Daub concluded by asking if I could perhaps

check this out.

I was reluctant, having pretty well ruined my eyes in the past year reading old newspaper accounts of UW boxing matches on microfilm. On the other hand, the Crazylegs nickname was so much a part of Elroy that its origin should be beyond any dispute.

How cool was the nickname? The cable sports network ESPN once did a ranking on its website of the best nicknames in the history of pro football, and Hirsch's Crazylegs was No. 1. The *Chicago Tribune* did a similar listing in 1989. In that one, Crazylegs ran second to Jack "the Assassin" Tatum of the Oakland Raiders. Trailing Crazylegs Hirsch were Gene "Big Daddy" Lipscomb of the Baltimore Colts, Dick "Night Train" Lane of the Detroit Lions, and "Mean" Joe Greene of the Pittsburgh Steelers.

Friday, I squinted into the microfilm machine to try to get a definitive answer on the origin of Crazylegs for Ed Daub. I did—I think.

One of the first things I learned was something of a shock. In that 1942 season—Hirsch's only college season with the Badgers—he had a nickname, all right. But it wasn't Crazylegs.

The front page of the *Capital Times* sports page for October 29, 1942—12 days after the Soldier Field game in which Elroy was allegedly nicknamed Crazylegs "from that day forward"—the headline said Hirsch had been hospitalized with a sore throat. There was a picture of Elroy under another headline: "'Ghost' Goes to Hospital." The photo caption read: "If there is any gloom in a highly optimistic Wisconsin football camp today, it's for a good reason. Elroy 'Ghost' Hirsch (above), the Badgers' explosive sophomore left halfback, Wednesday was confined to the university infirmary with a sore throat."

Hirsch's nickname was Ghost.

Apparently that stuck through most of the season. In recalling the 1942 season, my correspondent, Ed Daub, was right about the Badgers playing Missouri the week before they played the Great Lakes Naval Station. But he was wrong about the game ending in a tie. The UW–Missouri game was October 10, 1942, at Camp Randall. Here is the lead sports headline on the game from the *Capital Times*:

"Hirsch Roars! Badgers Topple Missouri, 17–9." Two photo headlines again trumpeted Ghost Hirsch: "Hirsch is a 'Ghost' . . . Just Ask Missouri." And "'The Ghost' Walks Again.'"

The following week, October 17 against Great Lakes Naval in Chicago, was supposedly the game when Hirsch was dubbed Crazylegs by Powers. No doubt Powers wrote that sentence which I quoted above, but it didn't stick, at least not in Madison, not then.

The November 1 *Cap Times* sports page had another headline after Hirsch helped the Badgers beat Ohio State 17–7 two weeks later: "'The Ghost' on the Loose—for 58 Yards."

The first mention of Crazylegs I found in any Madison paper came after the 1942 season, when sportswriter Harry Sheer of the *Capital Times* wrote approvingly of Hirsch's season and noted that Elroy was called "everything from Ghost to Crazylegs."

By the 1943 season, Ghost was gone, and so was Elroy. He had transferred to Michigan, and when the Badgers played the Wolverines November 13 in Ann Arbor, Hirsch was sidelined with a shoulder injury. The *Capital Times* noted that "Elroy (Crazy Legs) Hirsch was so determined to score against his old Wisconsin mates" that he substituted himself in and kicked an extra point in the 27–0 Michigan win.

By then, "the Ghost" was history. Maybe someone figured out that the nickname had already been bestowed on Red "the Galloping Ghost" Grange.

In any case, Crazylegs it was, and given what Powers wrote, Elroy was lucky. Somehow Elroy "Demented Duck" Hirsch doesn't quite fly.

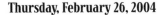

Thursday, February 26, 2004

"Spike" a Legendary Wrestler

The two men using the cover of darkness to liberate the safe from the Durfee Roofing Company on South Park Street had a problem. Not only could they not open the safe, which is bad enough when you are in the safecracking business, but neither could they lift it, to take it elsewhere for further study.

Fortunately, or unfortunately as it turned out, one of the men knew somebody who could. The two men, Kenneth and Louis Dickie, who were brothers, called in reinforcements in the person of Curtis "Spike" Peterson, a likable Mount Horeb native famous locally as a wrestler for Jimmy Demetral. Spike loved everything about wrestling except the paycheck.

"It seems all the money you make wrestling you pay to the court in fines," a judge, Edward Owens, told Peterson in November 1946. Spike was in for his 13th traffic violation in two years.

"Judge," he said, "all the money I make wrestling you could put in your eye."

It followed that when the Dickie brothers came calling two years later on the matter of the Durfee safe, Spike Peterson was interested.

This all started because there arrived the other day a press release for a new book, *Pile Driver: The Life of Charles "Midget" Fischer,* by Wisconsin writer Kenneth R. Boness. Fischer was a 1930s professional wrestler from Butternut, Wisconsin, north of Park Falls, and is credited with originating the "pile driver" move in wrestling, which, for the uninitiated, consists of holding a foe's head between your legs and driving him into the mat.

The new book was mentioned in passing to Joe "Buffo" Cerniglia, the well-known bon vivant, master of the Italian Workmen's Club, and walking encyclopedia of that erstwhile Madison neighborhood known as the Greenbush. Hearing the name Pile Driver, Cerniglia immediately recalled the Durfee safe job and Spike Peterson, whose nickname had originated as "Spike Driver" before being shortened.

"He could drive a spike through a two-by-four with his fist," Cerniglia said. "Oh, he was a great character. Everyone in Madison knew him. He used to raise rattlesnakes. I don't know how many times he got bit. He kept them in boxes behind a small grocery on Mound Street."

Cerniglia chuckled. "He was a lot smarter than he acted," he said.

Peterson was born in Mount Horeb in August 1911. He made up for his abysmal eyesight—he wore half-inch-thick glasses—by working hard on his physique. That led him to the wrestling ring, and his fame there led to publicity when he went to court, which was often.

In March 1948 the Madison papers touted him as "Robin Hood" because he kept getting busted for stealing coal from the railroad to give to people who couldn't afford to heat their homes. Railroad detectives caught him coming out of the Milwaukee Road's yard with $19 worth of coal. Ordered to appear before Judge Roy Proctor, Peterson—"a brawny member of Madison's wrestling fraternity," according to the *Capital Times* story the next day—arrived in court "with four bunches of carrots and a pot roast on his person."

Regarding the coal, Spike explained his charitable activities and said, "I got an oil burner in my own trailer so I don't need the coal."

Proctor gave him a 30-day suspended sentence. "And stay out of the coal business," the judge said.

"I guess I can restrain myself," Spike said.

He couldn't. Peterson was back in front of Proctor within a month. The police apprehended him in the act of delivering coal to a south side woman. Proctor gave him $10 or 10 days and Spike said he thought he could raise the money.

The Durfee safe job, a year later, was a bit more serious. "I was in bed at 12:30 a.m.," Peterson told the judge (Proctor again), "when the two Dickies stopped at the door. I didn't like to be disturbed at that time, but I got up and opened the door and the two lads came in. I asked what was up, and they said, 'Come on and get dressed.' And they said they were going down and do something at Durfee's."

In early December 1948, the Dickies got six months each and Peterson got 60 days. The week before Christmas, Spike posted a letter to the *Capital Times* from his residence in the Dane County Jail. The subject was the jail's cuisine, which Spike found lacking in good Wisconsin dairy products. The paper published his letter and a follow-up a week later, in which Spike thanked a local bowling league for delivering the following to jail: "A case full of good American cheese sandwiches, thick with cheese and butter, and a plate of pickles and an extra pound of butter for myself."

Out of jail, Spike returned to the wrestling ring, but his career was cut short. In May 1951, Peterson traveled to Richland Center for a match with Sam Abraham of Springfield, Illinois. At one point in the match Abraham lifted Peterson above his head and attempted an "airplane spin" move, which Peterson thwarted by struggling loose, only to land head first on the mat.

His neck was broken. A day later, Curtis "Spike" Peterson was dead. He was 39.

Monday, March 1, 2004

Three Steps to Fashion Recovery

The other day, in a major metropolitan East Coast newspaper, James Lipton, host of *Inside the Actors Studio* on Bravo, offered some insight into a problem that has haunted me my entire life.

Mr. Lipton, who does not suffer from an inferiority complex, took a moment from discussing his car (a Mercedes SUV) and his framed letter from Tom Cruise to reveal why he is a poor dresser. Of course, that's not the way Lipton phrased it to the *New York Times Sunday Magazine.* He said, "Sartorially, I am a disaster." That means he's a poor dresser.

Lipton then gave the reason why: "I have no taste. I am from Michigan. I am a Midwesterner with Midwestern taste."

I have never been what might be called a "natty" dresser. Years ago, and you can look it up, the Madison newspaper *Isthmus* was running some kind of special fashion section, and an editor asked if I would submit to a fashion makeover out at West Towne Mall, and then write about it.

I don't want to say the project was unsuccessful, but after working with me, half a dozen fashion consultants from various West Towne stores formed a support group to sort through the nightmarish experience. It was either that, they said, or get out of the business entirely.

I have three rules when it comes to fashion, or what I prefer to call "getting dressed."

1. Wear only white socks. Not only will this give you the virtue of consistency, it will keep you from getting upset when the washing machine or dryer mysteriously eats one sock out

of a pair, which happens weekly in every laundry room in America and is one of the greatest mysteries of the 20th century. What happened to the other sock? If all your socks are white, who cares?

2. Waistbands must be flexible. This keeps you from worrying about either losing or gaining weight, and as we all know, worrying is bad for you. If you put on a few pounds, your pants still fit. This also means that if you gain or lose some weight, you needn't run to the store to buy new pants, which in turn relieves you from the stress of shopping for clothes. In his biography of Ernest Hemingway, *Papa Hemingway*, A.E. Hotchner noted that the only two things Hemingway ever expressed fear about were public speaking and clothes shopping. Hotchner was with Hemingway in some fancy New York store when a clerk tried to sell Hemingway a suitcase that would hold nine suits. "Can afford suitcase," Hemingway said. "Can't afford nine suits."

3. Never wear a necktie. This ironclad rule has caused me a bit of trouble over the years, and I've broken it (exactly three times that I remember in the last 25 years), but it is a most worthwhile goal.

Some years ago, the *Washington Post* conducted a readers' survey, posing the question "Why Do Men Wear Neckties?"

The Post received a wide variety of responses, including this one: "Men wear neckties because other men wear neckties. There's a subservient quality to wearing a tie." And: "Men wear neckties because women wear high heels. It's a form of attire revenge that each gender practices on the other."

And finally, from a man named Jack Cuddihy of Hamburg, New York: "I am not a thin person, and when I take off my tie, but keep my suit on, my stomach appears much larger. It may be real or imagined but I look fatter without a tie. Because much of the developed world eats well, the large men are in no hurry to lose a piece of material that hides or draws attention away from something that we would rather not suck in all day."

Allow me to note that if Mr. Cuddihy would only observe the second of my three fashion rules and have a flexible waistband, he would not need to worry about sucking in his big gut, and he wouldn't need a necktie.

While my three rules of fashion have served me well over the years, there's no point denying that I've sometimes wondered about my minimal interest in clothes.

Now James Lipton has revealed the answer: I'm from the Midwest, so I have no taste.

I suppose some people might consider that Midwest-bashing, but I prefer to turn the other cheek, which is easier to do if you're not wearing a necktie.

It also reminds me of what one of the few actors who hasn't submitted to an interview with James Lipton once said to the great Michigan novelist Jim Harrison. Harrison had just cooked a fabulous and artery-bursting six-course dinner for a group of people at Jack Nicholson's house in California. At one point Nicholson grinned and said, "Only in the Midwest is overeating still regarded as an act of heroism."

Right on, Jack. And if you're dressed correctly, you won't even have to worry about letting your belt out a notch.

═══

Wednesday, March 17, 2004

Dr. Zorba Paster—Abducted!

The three men had masks and guns and spoke Spanish. In the predawn hours of a Sunday in Caracas, Venezuela, late last month, the men had braked their car to a stop on a highway exit ramp leading to the Caracas airport. The driver swung the car around to block the exit. The car following was forced to stop. In the passenger seat of the second car was Dr. Zorba Paster, the Madison physician well known for his many radio and TV appearances. Paster had been about to catch a flight back to Madison. What he got instead was a gun stuck against his right temple.

It was a nice morning," Paster was recalling Tuesday. "I had the car window open."

Paster saw the guns and masks and for an instant thought he was dreaming. Then he felt the gun and knew he was not.

Speaking publicly about his ordeal for the first time Tuesday in an interview, Paster said he had traveled to Caracas last month for a medical conference. He speaks often on the topic of chronic pain, and a couple of years ago, in New Jersey at a similar conference, a German colleague had approached Paster and said, when we come to Latin America, will you talk to us? Paster said he would.

The conference had gone well, and Paster was looking forward to the flight home, then a few days in his office here, and then another trip, this one to Australia for another talk, and then on to China, where Paster would meet his son's future-in-laws.

Now here he was a few miles from the Caracas airport with a gun to his head. In the driver's seat next to him, Paster's Venezuelan driver had begun shaking and crying.

Paster, who has studied Zen and Buddhism, swallowed hard and determined to remain calm. "I realized that right away," Paster said. "I figured, they want everything I have. Well, that's no problem. I put my hands up and kept them where they could see them. And I kept saying, 'No problem.' I wasn't happy, obviously, but I was calm."

There were three of them altogether. They wore masks but Paster determined that two of the men were in their 40s and one was younger, in his 20s. They were speaking Spanish and they forced Paster and his driver into the backseat. Two of the thugs got in the front seats of Paster's car and began following the third man, who drove off in the other car.

At which point Zorba Paster realized that he might die.

"I thought, 'They're hijacking me. This isn't good,'" Paster said. They drove for about 10 minutes into the hills and Paster began to think about his family, and how awful it would be for them if he died in this distant locale.

He forced those thoughts from his head. "I said to myself, 'Their goal is money. They haven't hurt me. They haven't really even touched me.' I kept my hands in view and made all my movements slowly."

His driver, meanwhile, huddled in back next to Paster, was still shaking and crying. "I'm sure they were saying some terrible things to him that I couldn't understand," Paster said. Paster called again on his Zen training, and his years of meditation, the idea having always been that if you can attain a state of calm in everyday life, you may find it when you most need it, in a time of crisis, as well. This was a crisis Paster never expected to see. He was calm.

"It was the one thing I could control," Paster said. "I could stay calm."

Finally, on the side of a hill overlooking the airport, the men pulled the car over and ordered Paster and his driver out. Again, a potentially bad sign. Maybe they didn't want to get blood on the car, which was valuable. Paster stayed calm.

Standing by the car, one of the men indicated he wanted Paster's wallet. Rather than reach for it himself, Paster allowed the masked man to reach into his pocket and take it. He then offered them his watch. It was a Timex, and the man threw it on the ground. Paster picked it up and handed it to him.

One of the men indicated Paster should disrobe. He refused. "It didn't seem proper," he said. They'd looked inside his pants for a money belt—what else could there be? The men didn't press it and pointed Paster and his driver back into the rear seat of the car. The two older thugs got back into their car. The younger man got into the front seat of Paster's car. He pointed his gun at Paster's face, and Paster again thought that he might die.

"Welcome to Venezuela," the man said, in English. He got out and climbed into the other car.

Paster and his driver sat for several minutes in silence. It was over. Paster had lost some $200 and, more important, his passport, but he was alive. He was alive.

At the airport, it was clear Paster wouldn't be getting on a plane without identification. He went back to the hotel, where his German host was upset to learn what had happened, and helped Paster get in touch with the U.S. Embassy in Caracas, which was closed on Sunday. Then, that night, the unbelievable happened again. A Caracas woman called Paster at his hotel. She had found his passport and pictures and belongings on the ground outside a restaurant. (Paster had carried a card identifying his hotel in case he forgot anything—that's how the woman knew where to find him.) A meeting was arranged. The woman returned his passport—and his visa to go to China in a few days. She wanted no reward. She had a son in Philadelphia. If Paster wanted to send her boy something nice, that would be fine.

"The kindness of strangers," Paster was saying this week.

He got back from China this past weekend, and said the trip was great. He has thought about his ordeal often. "Oddly," he said, "I don't feel any anger toward those men who robbed me." They had, after all, let him live. He thinks if there's a message for anyone else in what happened to him, it's that staying calm is the key. "You think you have no control but you do have control," he said. "You can remain calm."

On that note, when his plane for China laid over in San Francisco, Zorba Paster found a Zen center and made a donation. It seemed like the right thing to do.

━━━━━━

Wednesday, April 21, 2004

Rocky Rococo's Full Circle at 30

When Rocky Rococo, the pizza restaurant chain, celebrated its 30th anniversary earlier this month, co-founder Wayne Mosley kept it low-key.

"We went out to dinner and kind of took pleasure in it," Mosley was saying Tuesday of the April 4 anniversary. "Thirty years goes fast."

Rocky's is a great Madison story—you can bet Mosley and his co-founder, Roger Brown, shudder to think they almost called their first restaurant The Pizza Factory. The Rocky's saga includes ups and downs over three decades— including an ambitious attempt at national franchising in the 1980s—but the restaurants endure as a familiar landmark on the local scene. Successful restaurateurs like Monty Schiro and Craig Culver worked for Rocky's early in their careers. "When you see all the restaurants come and go," Mosley said, "we're happy to still be here."

Mosley and Brown first met at the University of Illinois in Champaign in the early 1970s. They'd grown up in Chicago not knowing each other, met through a mutual friend, and found out they had restaurants in common. Mosley had worked at restaurants through high school and was in law school primarily to appease his family. Brown was working at a Champaign pan pizza joint called Garcia's. The place was always packed.

Brown and Mosley began talking about opening their own pizza place, preferably on another Big Ten campus. The concept would borrow what they liked about Garcia's. Later,

128

the Garcia's owner told an advertising consultant, "I always knew Roger was going to do this because he was always walking around on my time taking notes."

It came down to locations in Madison and East Lansing, Michigan, and they liked the Madison deal better. The building was a small restaurant on Gilman Street just off State called Brown's Diner, owned by Orv Erickson and Darrell Cook. Brown convinced them that the blue plate specials served in the diner did not fit a college crowd. "We can do better," Brown said.

On the drive from Chicago to finalize the deal in Madison, Brown and Mosley starting kicking around names. Rocky Rococo came up early—it was the name of a character on an album by the Firesign Theater comedy troupe. Brown and Mosley weren't sure, though, and had pretty much decided on The Pizza Factory when at the last minute they flipped back to Rocky Rococo.

It was a stroke of genius because it let people know they were going to be different (Madison hadn't had pizza by the slice before), and when they created an actual Rocky character—a tough-talking gangster who was, deep down, a pizza-loving good guy—the good times really rolled. Their early TV spots were hilarious: one had Rocky dressed up in medical garb and saying, "Nine out of 10 doctors recommend my pizza and the tenth ain't recommending nothin' no more."

The Gilman Street restaurant had started slowly. There wasn't money for advertising and the competition was heated. Brown arrived one day to find a bullet hole in the restaurant's sign. Brown thought, *Someone shot our sign!* He climbed up with a knife to dislodge the bullet and received a shock. The hole was from faulty wiring.

Gilman Street gradually took off, but the key development came in 1975 when an ailing steak joint on State Street near Lake became available. It was a tremendous location, more visible than Gilman. Brown and Mosley didn't get it cheap but they got it, and they rode that State Street location like it was Secretariat.

It led to expansion into other Wisconsin cities and a short-lived partnership with the Oscar Mayer Corporation—eventually it led to franchising. There was large, even rabid, interest in Rocky's from all over the country. Rocky's sold its franchises by territory. A franchise owner would agree to put up X number of stores in X years in Texas, for instance. Rocky's was on the record anticipating 700 stores by 1990. Pizza Hut, take cover!

It didn't happen. There are all kinds of theories why, but the fundamental reason was that franchising is a perilous exercise. Away from Wisconsin, Rocky's had no name recognition. A distant franchisee needed half a dozen stores to make TV advertising viable, but if a first store wasn't doing well, the franchisee was reluctant to add more.

Also, franchisees seeing mediocre numbers were soon calling Madison with unsolicited menu advice. The Madison home base became top-heavy with executive talent lured for the anticipated boom. Worse, Brown and Mosley found themselves wearing suits and ties to the office—it wasn't fun anymore. A Chicago ad agency even suggested dumping the beloved Rocky character.

The fallout took several years, but in the end Brown and Mosley wound up selling Rocky's to a California company, with the agreement that the co-founders would retain control of several restaurants in and around Madison.

"We're franchisees of the company we founded," Mosley said this week, and that's fine with him. There are 45 Rockys total. Mosley and Brown today have eight restaurants in Madison, three in La Crosse, and one in Wisconsin Dells. They also still have that great character they dreamed up all those years ago, and Mosley said there's a photo shoot scheduled later this week with Rocky on a motorcycle. What 30-year-old doesn't want to ride a motorcycle?

―――――

Friday, April 30, 2004

The Fess: Full of Good Stories

When Rod Clark was working as a night clerk in the old Fess Hotel in the early 1970s, when it really was a hotel, his duties included watching the switchboard and patching guests who wanted to make a phone call through to an outside line.

One night, as Clark—today publisher of the esteemed literary magazine *Rosebud*—monitored the considerable variety of urban wildlife that wandered into the Fess after dark, a switchboard light started blinking. A guest was ringing the desk. The only problem was the call was originating from a room in an area of the hotel's third floor that Clark had been told was demolished for a parking ramp. Was a ghost calling? With some hesitance, Clark answered.

This story and others surfaced last summer when Clark lunched with his old friend John Tuschen, the former longtime poet laureate of Madison. In 1971, Tuschen and Clark spent a wonderfully strange year living in the "penthouse" suite of the Fess, which is now the Great Dane Brew Pub, off the Square on East Doty Street. Naturally, the site for the two friends' recent lunch was the Great Dane. The karma at lunch has now led Clark to write a wonderful piece about those days, "Fessing Up," that will appear in an issue of *Rosebud* this summer. A copy of the story was surreptitiously leaked to me this week.

The only problem with the piece from my view is that Clark gives scant attention to the Fess when it ceased being a hotel and became instead a restaurant and bar. "Later in

131

the '70s," Clark writes, "the Fess became an upscale eatery with elegant suites upstairs." One of those suites was the office of *Madison* magazine, where I worked. Having a great bar downstairs was a happy coincidence, and the late Jim Selk and I began trying to prove Warren Hinckle's famous observation that there is nothing in the job description of magazine editor that can't be accomplished in a saloon with a working telephone.

In its heyday—roughly the 1980s—the Fess at cocktail time was the best show in Madison. Paul and Sara Soglin had their first date there on New Year's Eve 1980. Jimmy Buffett showed up after a concert scheduled for the Columbus Motor Speedway washed out. The regulars included trial lawyers, strippers, politicians, reporters, judges, dope runners, and hustlers of every stripe. Things just seemed to happen at the Fess. I was having a drink at the bar with Gene Parks when he received, by carrier, the infamous letter firing him as Madison's affirmative action officer.

Of course, why should Rod Clark have written about those days? He had his own remarkable era to chronicle. Few people in the 1980s realized the Fess had until recently been a functioning hotel. Occasionally we would chuckle at the bar when people who had made a reservation at the Fess showed up with their suitcases. What were they thinking?

Well, they were thinking it was a hotel, which it was from when it was built, in the 1850s, until 1972. (Clark says the 1840s, and he may be right, but the late Peter Wright, who once owned a piece of the Fess, told me late 1850s.) In any case it is now a national historic landmark.

Clark's piece reveals that the Fess was pretty wild even before it became a bar. In 1971, the hotel had a coffee shop and no bar, so social service agencies would often book their clients into the Fess. It was after Clark and Tuschen upgraded to the penthouse suite that Rod took on night clerk duties to pay the extra rent.

As reported above, one night Clark found himself

behind the desk staring at a light blinking from a room that was said to no longer exist. When Clark picked up, an ancient male voice summoned him to the room for an errand. Clark climbed the stairs (there was no elevator) and with some difficulty found a secluded wing of the hotel he had not previously seen.

When Clark knocked, an old man in his pajamas shoved a $100 bill at him and issued marching orders for Clark to go immediately to a King Street bar and return with "a bottle of white port, a liverwurst sandwich, and a carton of Kents."

There is more to the story, and as it is Clark's and not mine, I'll not reveal it. You may look for it in *Rosebud* in August.

One thing Clark's piece did for me was get me thinking about how many good times with how many good people I shared at the Fess, even if they never could seem to serve a hot bowl of chili. The mix of people make a place, and for a while there no place mixed it up better than the Fess. I know there are other hot spots downtown now, but tonight I plan to get my Fess bar stool out of the garage— liberated on June 26, 1994, closing day—and toast those good old days.

———————

Wednesday, May 12, 2004

Rising Adventure, Dramatic Descent

Tuesday morning, I placed a call to the Rockland Psychiatric Center, which is located 18 miles north of New York City. I wanted to talk to a patient, a woman who is not there voluntarily.

I was transferred to several stations, and finally a nurse said, "You have to call the pay phone." She gave me the number.

I dialed it, and after a few rings, a woman answered. There was noise in the background.

"I'm trying to reach Jana Schneider," I said.

"I'm Jana."

For a long time, if you wanted to reach McFarland native Jana Schneider, 52, you would search the most glamorous addresses on Broadway, where in 1985 she received a Tony Award nomination for her role *in The Mystery of Edwin Drood.*

Later, after a stunning career change, you could find the former Miss Teen Wisconsin first runner-up and UW–Madison graduate in the world's hottest spots, where as a war photographer just this side (some said that side) of reckless she caught searing images of combat. In Bosnia in 1992, she also caught shrapnel in her legs and head. The wounds raised Schneider's profile, and soon you could find her in *People* magazine, and on the CBS show *Street Stories*, where she was interviewed by Ed Bradley.

This week, you can find Jana Schneider in the pages of the May 17 issue of *U.S. News & World Report* magazine, the subject of an extraordinary 4,200-word story by Kit R. Roane titled "A Fall From Grace." It was near the end of that magazine piece that I learned that Schneider is now a psychiatric patient involuntarily committed by a state court in New York.

"I really don't want to be here," Schneider told me Tuesday.

Fall from grace, indeed. As detailed by Roane, who is both a writer and photographer based in New York (and heard of Schneider's plight through a photography connection), Jana Schneider's story is that of a small-town girl whom the town could not contain.

Roane interviewed her brother, James, now in California: "My sister was an actress from age 2, and her most rave reviewer was her father."

Also interviewed was her UW drama professor, Robert Skloot: "She was a kind of independent free spirit, a forceful presence to contend with."

After UW–Madison she went to New York City and landed some small roles in touring shows, finally hitting in 1985 with *Edwin Drood*. There was an early, short-lived marriage, and when her *Drood* success didn't lead to more substantial roles, Schneider pulled a dramatic career switch: She became a combat photographer.

Roane writes that Schneider had "talked with the heads of photo agencies about how to break into the business and learned that the quickest path to success was to go where others feared to tread."

Not for nothing did an old boyfriend, when asked by Roane about Schneider's defining characteristic, reply: "She had no fear." Her visa stamps included Sri Lanka, Afghanistan, Iraq, and Bosnia. It was in Sarajevo in June 1992 that a blast from a Serbian tank killed the Slovenian journalist with whom Schneider was traveling. She was lucky to survive herself, and back in the United States, the wounds made her a celebrity of sorts. In January 1993 Schneider was visiting family around Madison and gave an interview to the *Capital Times* in which she said she thought her image was becoming too flamboyant.

"It's a bit like here's this woman who is breaking the normal middle-class rules concerning rape, sexuality, danger, and death," Schneider said. "I wish they would have concentrated on the humanitarian idealism which I observe to be constantly blocked by political corruption or hypocrisy."

In the decade since that interview, Schneider's world began to unravel. Roane's *U.S. News* piece tells of aborted projects—including a screenplay based on her life—along with the death of her father, a falling-out with her brother, and a growing paranoia that she was being watched.

Eventually Schneider's money ran out, and it was in December of last year that two New York City detectives found her sitting on a Manhattan stoop with a cigarillo between her lips, $1.91 in her pocket, and a plastic bag in her hand containing her worldly possessions. The cops took her to Bellevue, the famed New York psychiatric hospital, and from Bellevue she was transferred to her present location, the Rockland Psychiatric Center outside of the city.

"I'm trying to get back to Wisconsin," she said, when we spoke Tuesday by phone. On medicine for depression and possible schizophrenia, Schneider sounded articulate and focused. She apologized for a slight slurring of her words. "I've lost teeth," she said. "I lived for a while on a $1 box of Domino sugar."

Her hope is that family or friends in the Madison area will offer lodging or monetary assistance, which, her New York attorney, Michael Genkin, told me Tuesday, would make it more likely that either the Rockland staff or a New York court would allow her release. "Some means of community support would help," Genkin said.

Jana Schneider and I spoke for about 20 minutes, and at the end I wished her good luck.

"Thank you for calling," she said.

I heard from a third party that a few weeks after this column appeared, Jana got out of the hospital and came back to the Madison area. I asked the person to pass along my best wishes to Jana and say if she wanted to speak again for publication, she should get in touch. So far, she hasn't.

≡≡≡

Friday, June 18, 2004

Neviaser's Circle Grew and Grew

The second to last time I spoke with Dan Neviaser, he promised to get me Doug Moe's phone number.

That is not as strange as it sounds, but like a lot of things in the life of Neviaser, who died here Wednesday at 81, there's a story behind it. Neviaser liked stories and making connections, and no one in Madison had a more extensive rolodex. It held the names and numbers of the rich and famous, but it also included street characters and people down on their luck whom Neviaser, who made a fortune in a variety of businesses, never failed to help.

"He was always expanding his circle," Danielle Dresden was saying Thursday. Dresden is an award-winning playwright whose father, Max Dresden, was a famed physicist. Dresden came to Madison for college in the 1970s, and one day her phone rang and it was Neviaser, who introduced himself and was most friendly, though Dresden couldn't imagine why he was calling her.

"It turned out he knew my half-brothers in Virginia," Dresden said.

That's where Dan grew up, with no silver spoon. He never knew his father and helped his mother run a small business. He got into the University of Maryland mainly because he could play baseball. He came to Wisconsin as national sales manager for the Carnes Corporation.

In 1968 he went out on his own, with no real game plan or money. What he did have was considerable—energy, ambition, street smarts, and a bit of luck. Neviaser shared basement office space on Gorham Street with another young comer named David Carley. Together, they helped bring cable TV to Madison, and Dan would recall selling hook-ups door to door.

Through the cable business he met Jim Fitzgerald of Janesville, later to own the Milwaukee Bucks but then a successful developer of hotels and motels. Neviaser began developing hotels—including the campus Howard Johnson's here—as well as office buildings and retail malls, becoming in the process a consummate deal maker.

A couple of years ago, my phone rang one morning. It was Dan Neviaser.

"What are you doing for lunch?"

"Nothing."

"Yes, you are," Neviaser said. "You're having lunch with me at Tony Frank's. I'll be downstairs in 20 minutes."

I knew mine was not to reason why. He was speaking at the UW School of Business that afternoon, and maybe he wanted a warm-up audience. We knew each other reasonably well. I went to junior high with Dan's son, Bruce, and the Neviasers lived across the street in Hill Farms from Dick McKenzie, whose son Tim was a good friend of mine growing up. Dan Neviaser's first development was three apartment buildings in Verona with Dick McKenzie. This is a small town, let me tell you.

At the restaurant in 2002, Neviaser talked about his unlikely friendship with Paul Soglin, who was a long-haired downtown alderman when they met. Neviaser was developing the Johnson Street HoJo's, and Soglin wrote a column attacking him in the *Daily Cardinal*. Driving on Mifflin Street that day, Neviaser spotted his antagonist walking on the sidewalk. "I'm the guy you attacked in the newspaper," Neviaser said. "Can I give you a lift?"

Soglin got in and said, "If my friends see me riding with you they'll go crazy."

"Not as crazy as mine if they see me with you,"

Neviaser said.

Later, they found common ground and mutual respect. Danielle Dresden called Dan "Madison's good-hearted capitalist," and when Soglin was first elected mayor in 1973 he made Neviaser one of his first committee appointments.

He said his talk at the business school was to be on the art of negotiation. He would give the students anecdotes and a few rules that had served him well in a lifetime of closing deals: Find common ground to break the ice, and always have a line in your mind that you will not cross.

As we left the restaurant he spoke of how proud he was of his wife and kids, and since he knew I knew Bruce, he laughed and said he wasn't sure Bruce was going to make it in the business world, now that he had at long last decided to join his dad in the family business. Bruce was 45 minutes late for the first meeting his dad set up for him. "If you weren't my son, I'd fire you," Dan said. Bruce learned, and now has a vastly successful company that builds and operates water parks. "When I flew up to Mayo for my annual physical," Dan said, "I flew in Bruce's plane." It was at a later medical appointment that Dan learned he had a particularly bad cancer.

The diagnosis was some months off when we last spoke. I had an idea that I wanted to write a column about the former Denver Nuggets pro basketball coach, Doug Moe, a column that for obvious reasons might be funny. I called the Nuggets and never heard back. Maybe they thought it was a crank, but then I called Dan Neviaser, who through Fitzgerald had good pro basketball contacts.

A day later, I got a voice mail from Dan, who was traveling. "I'm in Florida but I'm working on it."

The next morning, he called again. "I have Doug Moe's cell phone number," Dan Neviaser said.

I was, you may guess by now, not surprised.

Saturday, July 17, 2004

Hope and Doom on Interstate 26

The first time Chuck Stiles set eyes on Alicia May Goodwin, she couldn't have looked more lost. This was last Sunday afternoon in North Carolina.

"She was dragging her suitcase on the shoulder of the road," Stiles, a Wisconsin-based long-distance truck driver, was saying Thursday night in a telephone interview.

By Tuesday, Goodwin, 27, knew where she wanted to go. "I'd like to see Madison," she said.

In the summer, Stiles, 47, who lives outside Kenosha, has his 12-year-old son, Matt, with him in his truck. There was no way Matt was going to let his dad not stop on Sunday, when they spotted Goodwin walking by the highway in the pouring rain.

In the next couple of days they covered 800 miles and much of their lives, swapping stories. Matt and Alicia played movies and video games in the truck, and Stiles, who had lived and worked in Madison, said he thought Goodwin would enjoy the city's free-spirited atmosphere. It's an artistic city, Stiles said. The young woman agreed it sounded promising. When Stiles turned his truck around and headed back for Wisconsin, Goodwin was on board.

Goodwin was a free spirit, all right. "Free spirit is what we would say about her all the time," Goodwin's mother, Patricia Wallace, told the State newspaper of Columbia, South Carolina, this week. "She would travel, and we would not hear from her for months and months."

It was outside Asheville, North Carolina, on Interstate

40, that Chuck and Matt Stiles first spotted Goodwin walking in the rain. She later told Matt she didn't have her thumb out because a short time earlier, some guys in a car had pretended to stop and then threw pizza at her.

When Stiles stopped his truck at Matt's urging, Goodwin agreed to a ride. "She was a little standoffish at first," Stiles said. As the hours passed, the young woman became more animated. She would skip from topic to topic and occasionally get a faraway look in her eye. At one point she said she had been involved with the occult, though she was wearing a crucifix around her neck. A moment later she was singing a Madonna song. She warmed up to Matt, and soon they were playing video games. And Stiles talked to her about Madison.

Once, when Goodwin was sleeping, Matt said to his dad, "She goes through some odd spells."

Stiles, who is a devout Christian, told his son, "We are going to try to help her, and we are going to pray for her."

After Stiles dropped his cargo in South Carolina and reloaded, they stopped and bought Goodwin some new clothes. "A simple black dress," Stiles said.

Sometime after midnight on Tuesday, with the truck near Columbia, South Carolina, and headed north, a powerful thunderstorm caused Stiles to pull his truck off the highway into a rest area on Interstate 26.

"I'm going to get some sleep," Stiles said. His truck has two bunks. He doesn't let Matt leave the truck while he's sleeping, but Goodwin said she was going to go outside, smoke a cigarette, and read a book.

"She pointed to a picnic table," Stiles said. "She said, 'I'll be right there.'"

Stiles said, "She had on the dress we bought her." Before she stepped outside, he said, she kissed the crucifix.

The trucker is not sure how long he slept. An hour or two, not much more. But he woke to the sound of sirens and commotion and the news that the highway had been closed because of an accident.

"Where's Alicia?" Stiles asked his son, who had been napping as well.

The boy didn't know, and Stiles got out of the truck.

Somebody said, "A woman got hit."

It was Alicia May Goodwin.

On the grassy median between the westbound and eastbound highways, emergency medical personnel were attending to an injured person. The South Carolina Highway Patrol had taken a call at 4:20 a.m. Tuesday. A two-person Newberry County ambulance crew arrived first and made the decision that Goodwin's injuries, including a broken leg, dictated she should be taken by helicopter to a trauma center.

Stiles reached the median as the helicopter was lifting off. In the confusion he tried to find out what happened, and already there were different versions. The young woman had told the medical team that she had been hit by a truck. She told someone else she had been hit by a car. There did not seem to be eyewitnesses, though several people recalled seeing her walking back and forth from the median to the rest area. A woman told Stiles she had seen Goodwin "crying in the bathroom." On Friday, the Columbia newspaper reported Goodwin had been struck "by a hit-and-run driver."

When the helicopter arrived, there was a crew of three inside: the pilot, Bob Giard; a nurse, Glenda Frazier Tessnear; and a flight paramedic, David Bacon. It was foggy in the predawn. Stiles saw the helicopter lift off.

"I didn't see what happened," he said later. "But I heard it."

What he heard was the helicopter crashing into a forest some 1,000 yards from the rest area. "A trooper was yelling they had just lost the helicopter," Stiles said. "I ran off in the direction it was headed."

There was nothing anyone could do. All four of the people in the helicopter were dead. The Columbia paper said it may be months before investigators can say with any certainty what happened.

Thursday night, Stiles and his son were back in Kenosha, trying to come to terms with what they had just experienced.

Friday, they were back in the truck, headed again for South Carolina.

"We're going to be with Alicia's mom," he said.

═══════════

Thursday, August 19, 2004

Mister Giblin Has Left the Room

It hardly seems possible that a colorful old Madison character named John Giblin got away earlier this year without anyone noticing, but the irrefutable evidence came Wednesday with a call to the Dane County coroner's office.

"He died March 18th."

"Does it say how old?"

"Seventy-four."

Well, hell.

I had last talked to Gib, as everyone called him, about five years ago when our mutual friend Wally Rhodes, the local travel impresario, died. Gib, who spoke warmly of his old friend Rhodes—"the most generous guy I ever knew"— was living then with another old crony, Ted Cosmides.

At one time or another, and sometimes in partnership, these guys owned bars that became meeting places for Madisonians of a certain ilk, mostly those who did not punch a nine to five clock. The places had names like The Newsroom, The Salad Bar, and Mr. Giblin's, a nonexclusive club that you joined by telling a joke and buying a round. Members were not preoccupied with longevity, and indeed, Cosmides died a year after Rhodes. Gib wound up in a rest home, saying if he had known he would live so long he would have taken better care of himself.

As I heard it, John Giblin first came to Madison from the east coast in the early 1950s to attend UW–Madison. The first mention of him in the Madison papers came in November 1956, when he answered a "Man on the Street" question in the *Capital Times* about fining juveniles who break the law. Giblin was identified as living at 614 University Avenue and working as a bartender.

His answer to the question was somewhat instructive: "I don't think the levying of fines is a good idea. It is far better to show the children how they were wrong, and try to help them do better in the future."

No doubt Gib felt the same way after undercover cops wiretapped his phone and eventually charged him with eight counts of commercial gambling.

That was still some years off when Giblin first found his way into Joe Troia's steakhouse and nightclub in the 600 block of State Street. Troia, a 1942 Central High grad who ran a number of restaurants in the city over the years, hired Giblin as a bartender.

It was a great hire. Giblin was a born storyteller, loved the bar business, and before too long opened his own saloon, Mr. Giblin's Club, on West Gilman Street. The location became notorious 25 years later as Jocko's, which was shut down by a federal drug probe.

Giblin's Club was famous, too, first for winning an award from the parent company of Crown Royal whiskey, which sent a vice president to Madison to tell Giblin his bar was selling more Crown Royal than any other establishment in the Midwest. Regulars knew how that came about. Gib was a Crown Royal man himself, and frequently thirsty.

That was fun, but Gib got some less welcome

attention in September 1971. A banner page one *State Journal* headline screamed, "State Team Arrests 2 in Gambling Crackdown; Giblin Club Operator Is Charged."

A search warrant had produced spread sheets, betting lines, and a gun with its serial number filed off. There were also tapes from the phone wiretaps, and the government came to the inescapable conclusion that Giblin was taking sports bets over his bar. In hindsight, it hardly seems shocking. You can still find parlay cards in Madison bars, and is there any business anywhere—forget bars—where a bracket for the NCAA basketball tournament doesn't circulate? Gib's attorney insisted the bets were "personal wagers" and ridiculed the state justice department for harassing his client. In the end Gib plea-bargained it down to a $200 fine and misdemeanor probation.

Giblin bounced back from that, and when Wally Rhodes opened his Newsroom saloon on Park Street, Gib ran the bar. When Wally died I tracked Gib down—he was still in Madison—for a word about his friend. "He loved life," Giblin said of Rhodes. Gib laughed and added, "He was the biggest tipper I ever met."

It was a couple of years later that I heard a nice story about an old pal of Gib's, Steve Badalich, setting him up in Bradenton, Florida, where Badalich had a house. Badalich is a highly successful retired businessman, formerly with UW Provisions, and the onetime owner of the Madison Capitals hockey team. He has homes in the Twin Cities and Bradenton and many good memories of playing cribbage and sipping whiskey with John Giblin.

When I located Badalich, however, he said that while he had indeed visited Giblin in the rest home in Madison and invited him down to Florida, Gib had declined. "I don't play golf," Gib grumbled.

His health was failing him, and he was grumpy—but a story from the old days could still make him smile. Like the time Gib's attorney became outraged at the weak testimony of a justice department agent who said he had tried to make a bet undercover at Giblin's. The attorney, indignant, said, "This man doesn't know the difference between a bet and a banana!"

He left us with a smile, too, or at least I'm grinning as I look over what I've written and realize when he died. Leave it to Gib to have made one last St. Patrick's Day.

═══════════

Tuesday, August 31, 2004

Recalling (Gulp) Cowboy Eddie

In full innocence the other day, a reader got in touch wondering if I know what has become of Cowboy Eddie.

My correspondent had no way of knowing that I have been trying to forget Cowboy Eddie for close to 40 years now.

Madison residents of a certain vintage will need no introduction to Eddie, who for 11 years sat at the hand of Howie Olson while Olson hosted a TV show for kids in Madison titled *Circus 3*. It ran daily throughout the 1960s on Channel 3 and an estimated 13,000 kids appeared on the program.

There's no question that the star of the show was Cowboy Eddie. Olson was a ventriloquist and Eddie was a wooden dummy.

Everyone was supposed to love Eddie, and I guess many people did, especially kids. I thought he was creepy.

It wasn't until I reached adulthood—actually, it wasn't until I got the recent e-mail about Cowboy Eddie—that I learned there is actually a phobia associated with a fear of ventriloquists' dummies. It is cleverly referred to as ventriloquist's dummy phobia—or automatonophobia.

I also found on the Internet the "24-Hour Phobia Clinic" promising to rid me of the phobia "fast, with no drugs and no awful 'exposure' therapy. . . . Feel better about yourself minutes from now. Rebuild your confidence, strength and long-term happiness. Regain the respect of your loved ones, friends and colleagues. Take control of the thoughts and emotions that caused ventriloquist's dummy phobia."

Well, it hasn't really been quite that life-altering. I think it may actually predate my attendance in the studio audience of *Circus 3*. In May 1962 that great TV series *The Twilight Zone* ran an episode written by Rod Serling titled "The Dummy," in which a ventriloquist's dummy stages a coup and ends up running the act. That episode gave me nightmares, and it was a few years later that I came face to face with Cowboy Eddie.

Most of Madison loved Eddie. *Circus 3* aired after school, and the upside of being in the studio audience was you got some of the first McDonald's hamburgers and Hostess Twinkies ever served here—they sponsored the show.

Howie Olson had moved to the city in 1957. His father had been a ventriloquist in vaudeville under the name The Great Chesterfield, and Eddie was his first dummy. Howie performed with the duo as a boy and later inherited Eddie. Olson had a show for kids in Houston for 14 years before coming to Madison.

One of Olson's young fans when *Circus 3* was having its run here was local writer Jay Rath, who told me Monday that he happened to be in the city room of the *Capital Times* when word came that Howie Olson had died in Florida. It was June 26, 1992.

Rath was drafted to write the obituary. In it, Rath noted that in 1984 Olson had told him he'd made arrangements to donate Eddie to the Wisconsin Historical Society, at the suggestion of Olson's friend, the great ventriloquist Edgar Bergen.

During that 1984 visit, Rath learned that Olson was

carving more dummies, holding workshops, and otherwise staying active as a ventriloquist. Also on that visit, Jay had a chance to hold Cowboy Eddie.

"He was heavier than heck," Rath told me. "Carved from oak. But a kind and gentle soul."

I'll take your word for that, Jay. He made a good first impression. Give him a few days and he might go *Twilight Zone* on you.

Flash forward a decade or so from Olson's death in 1992. Rath found himself wondering how Cowboy Eddie was doing in his new home at the Historical Society.

But when he called then-director George Vogt, Vogt could find no record of the society having received Eddie. Vogt had his staff check again. Again, no Eddie.

There you go. The dummy escaped. My first guess is that he's hosting a talk radio show here under a different name.

But Rath did a little more digging. As Jay wrote in a piece that you can now access at www.tvparty.com, "It was now a missing persons case—sort of—but there were a few clues." Rath found one of Olson's former students, "and through him I found another, Jacki Manna Read."

In the end, Olson had donated Eddie not to the Wisconsin Historical Society but to Read. Rath tracked Read down in Florida.

"How's Eddie?" Rath asked.

"He's great," Read replied. "I just had him refurbished by some very well-known puppet makers, and they do work with antique figures."

Rath told me Monday that when he last communicated with Read, she told him she was still doing shows with Eddie in Florida. I guess it's good that the dummy is doing well. Doing well—and 1,000 miles from here.

Thursday, September 9, 2004

Tale of Ovens Founder Intriguing

Last Saturday I mentioned that the Associated Press had taken note of L'Etoile's Odessa Piper in a feature distributed on the AP national features wire.

One sentence in the article particularly caught my attention: Piper "moved to Wisconsin to work with the late JoAnna Guthrie, owner of an organic farm and restaurant, and has never left the state."

I hadn't realized that Guthrie had died, and could find no mention of it in the archives of the daily newspapers, so maybe many of you didn't know, either.

It may be you've never even heard her name. But if you have been in Madison for any length of time, you have felt her influence.

Guthrie founded the Ovens of Brittany restaurant, and from the Ovens, now gone, sprang restaurants such as L'Etoile, the Wilson Street Grill, and others too numerous to count. The list of Ovens alumni reads like a restaurant business all-star team. Monty Schiro, whose numerous Food Fight restaurants include Johnny Delmonico's and the Eldorado Grill, spent years at the Ovens.

Guthrie, the original Ovens guru, was an energetic, charismatic, mysterious, and ultimately tragic figure.

She came to the Madison area in either the late 1960s or early '70s—published accounts vary—having grown up in Springfield, Ohio, where her parents worked for B.F. Goodrich.

Guthrie, too, worked for the rubber company, but only

149

briefly. She married a Venezuelan, moved to South America, met and befriended Winthrop Rockefeller, moved to New York, moved back to Ohio and became a TV weathercaster, and finally moved to Chicago, where her third husband was president of an Eastern religion-influenced group called the Theosophical Society.

The society still exists, and I found this definition of theosophy on its website: "Theosophy is the shoreless ocean of universal truth, love, and wisdom, reflecting its radiance on the earth, while the Theosophical Society is only a visible bubble of that reflection. Theosophy is divine nature, visible and invisible, and its Society human nature trying to ascend to its divine parent. Theosophy, finally, is the fixed eternal sun, and its Society the evanescent comet trying to settle in an orbit to become a planet, ever revolving within the attraction of the sun of truth."

No, I don't get that, either. And you may wonder what it has to do with croissants or morning buns or the Ovens of Brittany.

Just this: Guthrie and her husband bought a farm near Gays Mills as a base to advance the society's teachings, and when the marriage failed, Guthrie bought a house on Kendall Avenue in Madison and a building at 305 State Street that on March 23, 1972, opened as the Ovens of Brittany.

It was different from the start—a French restaurant spotlighting locally grown food and cooking from scratch in the land of steakhouses and supper clubs. It was different, too, because Guthrie's philosophical beliefs also played a role in the restaurant.

For a 1996 *Madison* magazine article, writer Judith Kirkwood interviewed Piper and several others who were there in the early years of the Ovens, which within a decade would become truly legendary in Madison and beyond.

One of them, Karen McKean, told Kirkwood, "Joanna's philosophy of bringing Eastern belief systems into Western culture was groundbreaking. At a time when young people

150

were feeling so rebellious that they wanted to tear down our society, she was talking about cultural transformation—new designs for living that reflected art and spirit."

The philosophy was printed on the back of the menu, and stories circulated about some odd kitchen rules, such as forbidding cooks to look directly into mixing bowls or the women on staff to part their hair—either would dissipate energy. Piper told Kirkwood, "I wouldn't want to wreck these wild stories by verifying or denying them. They were part of the mythology of the early years."

It was in those years that Piper and her colleagues invented the croissant (well, introduced it here, anyway) and the morning bun. Guthrie, however, was losing her way—sinking into an illness that would eventually be diagnosed as schizophrenia.

She eventually returned to Ohio, where she was in and out of treatment for the disease. Subsequent articles about the Ovens—and there were many, including one in the *Washington Post*—chronicled the restaurant's growth (the Ovens opened in several more locations) and, eventually, its demise.

Guthrie's presence hovered throughout those stories, though there was little concrete information about her condition. Her son, Rob Ibarra, was a UW–Madison vice chancellor in 1996 when he told Kirkwood that his mother was in Ohio and suffering delusions. Ibarra subsequently left Madison, taking a job at the University of New Mexico.

Looking on the internet, I found a February 2000 *Isthmus* story by Judy Davidoff (now with the *Capital Times*) that brought Guthrie's story to a conclusion. She had died a month earlier, in an Ohio nursing home, at 77. Her son said they wanted to scatter her ashes on a farm.

Rob Ibarra told me later his mother's ashes were scattered amid the beautiful Sandia Mountains in New Mexico.

Tuesday, October 19, 2004

Teetotaling Bar Owner: No Swearing in Here
Missouri Tavern Proprietor Hits 100

Mae Mefford was 50 years into the tavern business before she drank her first beer.

This was maybe eight years ago, at a wedding reception near Wisconsin Rapids.

"Somebody set a beer down in front of me," Mae was recalling Monday. "I'm conservative, you know. I don't want to waste anything. After it sat there a while I drank it down in three gulps."

Right about then a young man came up and asked her to dance. "It was wonderful," she said. "We danced a polka and he was up on his toes like you're supposed to be. I think he was the best dancer I ever saw."

She paused. "Maybe it was the beer."

Mae Mefford, who turned 100 years old on October 8, hasn't had a beer since. She sparkles without it. She's been running the Missouri Tavern, between Middleton and Sauk City on U.S. 12, for 64 years and still isn't sure she likes the tavern business. She likes the people who stop by, and the piano in the corner on which she plays from memory everything from "The Missouri Waltz" to "On Wisconsin." But she doesn't care for alcohol and she doesn't smoke, and if you swear under her roof you will be shown the door— even if it means she has to lock up for the night.

On Monday she unlocked the tavern door about mid-morning. It's her home, too. She sat on a chair near a large wood-burning stove.

Sunday had been a big day. Her friends and family had thrown a 100th birthday bash for her at the Springfield Town Hall, a couple miles up U.S. 12. People came from all over. Now on Monday she was going through a huge stack of cards and speaking with wonder of all the flowers and balloons and cake she'd brought home.

On the wall behind the bar were happy birthday wishes from George W. Bush and James Doyle. You're only 100 once, after all, and the fact is, Mae is kind of famous. John Kass wrote a column about her in the *Chicago Tribune* a couple of years ago, on her dislike of profanity, and that got Paul Harvey talking about her on the radio. "The Jay Leno show called the other day," Mae said. "I'm not sure if I'll be on or not."

She took a fall six weeks ago and is moving a bit slower than she would like, but Mefford's mind is still excellent. She likes to talk about the time she was in a horse and buggy with her dad, a South Dakota farmer, and they looked to the sky and there was Halley's comet. "The purest, whitest light I had ever seen," she said. Of course, she hadn't seen much. It was 1910 and Mae was 6 years old. "My father said maybe I would see it the next time around, in 75 years."

She remembers working hard in those South Dakota fields as a kid, and the day when the church bells a few miles away in Vermillion wouldn't stop ringing. "World War I had ended," she said.

She finished high school, married, and followed her husband, Albert "Missouri Al" Mefford, to Wisconsin. They both worked at Mendota State Hospital here for a time, but Al wanted to run a bar. They built the Missouri Tavern in 1940. "It's a well-built building," Mae said. "It's been hit four times by cars careening off Highway 12."

She has owned it alone since Al died in 1964. Only

days after his death, Mae's mother suffered a debilitating stroke. She appeared destined for a rest home, but Mae wouldn't have it. There was plenty of room in the rear of the tavern, and Mae took care of her for six years.

These days the tavern is usually open, but Mae locks up occasionally to go to church, and of course she closed Sunday afternoon so she could attend her party. Her neighbors and a couple of police officer friends stop often, just checking to make sure all is well. She likes to see them and, most of all, she likes to see young people. "I try to learn something new every day," she said.

It doesn't leave much time for regrets, and if Mae Mefford has one it's only remembering a low time in her life when she found herself wondering if she had the strength to go on. She found the strength, and more than that, found that even big problems tend to diminish with time. "I'm so happy I'm alive," she said.

It was when her mother got sick that Mae first learned to play the piano. She remembered her dad, who always seemed happy, coming in from a day in the field, tired but grinning. He'd wipe some sweat from his forehead and reach for her mom, dancing her around the house to "Meet Me in St. Louis."

That song was from the World's Fair in 1904, the year Mae was born. She played it Monday, on the piano in the Missouri Tavern, though it was clear that in her mind's eye she was somewhere else: The last century was young, Mae's parents were dancing and the music would never end.

Wednesday, November 3, 2004

"Thanks for the Use of the Hall"

A giant left the stage Tuesday.

I'm not referring to any of the politicians who won or lost. They come and go. I'm talking about Jimmy Breslin, who for over 40 years has been writing a passionate, funny, infuriating, and never dull newspaper column in New York City.

"I invented this column form," Breslin wrote Tuesday in Newsday, with typical swagger. "I now leave."

Regular visitors to this space know I am a big Breslin guy. I'd quote him more often except when I do, his lines are always the best thing in the column.

Not long ago I did a column on a Madison-based insurance investigator who had helped federal agents break up a sophisticated car insurance fraud ring in Chicago. I mentioned one of Breslin's stock column characters, Marvin the Torch, who burned down buildings for the insurance money but resisted being called an arsonist. "I build empty lots," Marvin said.

After that ran, I heard from the wonderful Madison poet John Tuschen, who said he hadn't been laughing much lately, but Breslin's line about Marvin had cracked him up.

It's like what Breslin once wrote about an earlier urban scribe, Damon Runyon: He put a smile into the newspaper, which usually has as much humor as a bus accident.

Breslin was often funnier than Runyon. So many pundits have written about the pros and cons of political polling. Reading them is like watching someone wring his hands. A month ago Breslin began his column like this:

"I am writing this in my office when the phone makes me jump. I reach for it. But the phone isn't making the sound. It is Pugsley the Parrot, who is in the corner of the office and imitates the phone ringing. He does it just about perfect.

"Now he cried:

"'Bush! Kerry. Kerry.'

"He is my poll. My poll is based on how many times Pugsley the Parrot calls out a candidate's name. He gets that from endlessly listening to people. Whichever candidate they talk about the most will be the one Pugsley the Parrot calls out the most.

"He is going to call this election. . . . I trust him. He is not some student in a sweatshirt sitting on a phone and then giving CBS, NBC, ABC, and the *New York Times* figures they regard as real. Pugsley the Parrot is no kid. These parrots live for 80 and 90 years.

"'Bush,' he says.

"Then he slips in a 'Stop abortion!'

"He obviously has had strict Roman Catholic owners."

Breslin's column started in the early 1960s in the *New York Herald Tribune*, now defunct. He had written a breezy book about the hapless New York Mets called *Can't Anybody Here Play This Game?* The paper excerpted the book, and when the excerpts were finished the author was asked to write a regular column about the city.

Breslin may not have "invented the form," as he claimed Tuesday, but he sure as hell shot life into it. Before Breslin, newspaper columnists tended to be either gossips or navel-gazers who never left the office. Breslin sat on bar stools and climbed tenement stairs and listened to the voices of New York. He found humor in the city's hard knocks, as in the early column about his friend who one night didn't realize there was a citywide blackout—he just assumed the electric company had shut off his power again.

Later, as the column moved to the *New York Daily News*

and finally *Newsday*, Breslin complained it was getting harder to be funny. The colorful rogues on the street had been replaced by ciphers who sold crack to teenagers. So he wrote about race and poverty and the duplicity of too many politicians.

Was he perfect? Of course not. In a business where job one is getting it right, Breslin sometimes didn't, and he was never quick to admit a mistake. But he got up every morning thinking of how best to comfort the afflicted and afflict the comfortable on his newspaper page, and he did that longer, and better, than anyone. Into his 70s, he wrote three columns a week until the end.

In this election season, he was tougher than anyone on George W. Bush. Breslin considered the war in Iraq a monstrous mistake, and he devoted more than one column to a simple list of the names of the young Americans killed in action.

In Tuesday's column, he brashly predicted a big Kerry victory. Reading this, you should know if he was right—though whatever happens, Jimmy Breslin's legacy is secure.

He ended on Tuesday with this: "Thanks for the use of the hall." It's the rest of us who should say thanks.

Wednesday, November 17, 2004

Madison Airman—A Lost Hero?

More than half a century after he disappeared, presumed dead, into either the Pacific Ocean or the harsh high mountains of British Columbia, someone is calling Ted Schreier a hero.

Surrounded by Reality

It's a story that not even his family knew, and because of what it involves—an Air Force training exercise gone wrong, and the possible loss of the radioactive plutonium core of a nuclear bomb—it's a story still sheathed in speculation and mystery.

Friday night on the Discovery Channel, Canadian filmmaker Michael Jorgensen will make the case that in February 1950, Capt. Theodore F. Schreier, who was from Madison, risked and ultimately lost his life in a single-handed attempt to keep U.S. nuclear weaponry and secrets from falling into enemy hands. The documentary is called *Lost Nuke*, and it promises to be a stunner.

Schreier was born in Cashton, east of La Crosse, and came to school at UW–Madison in 1936. With his wife, Jean, he had a home on the north side of Lake Mendota. Ted's parents, Mr. and Mrs. Fred Schreier, lived in Middleton, and Ted had a brother, Ernest Schreier, who also lived in Middleton.

Ted was a career Air Force officer, and in 1950 he was temporarily stationed in Fort Worth, Texas. On the night of February 13, Schreier was part of a crew of 17 scheduled to fly from Fairbanks, Alaska, to Fort Worth aboard a B-36 aircraft—a larger plane than the 747 of today.

The Air Force called it a routine training mission, but in fact it was a simulated nuclear "attack" on San Francisco, something that was done with some regularity during the Cold War. After completing the "attack," the plane would fly to Texas. A Mark 4 atomic bomb—"the most advanced nuclear weapon in America's growing atomic arsenal," according to a later story in the *Edmonton Journal*—was on board the B-36.

Some six hours into the flight, the plane encountered heavy rains, and then ice on its wings. An engine sputtered and burst into flames. Soon three engines were burning.

That much is not in dispute. The mystery is over what happened next. As the *Edmonton Journal* noted in 2000, "To this day, the details of what happened during the next 25 minutes . . . continue to be shrouded in Cold War secrecy and speculation."

It was originally reported that all 17 crew members had parachuted out of the plane. Twelve were found alive by fishing boats and the Canadian Navy, off the coast of British Columbia. The remaining five, including Ted Schreier, were presumed drowned.

No mention was made then of a bomb having been aboard, but six months later, the Air Force issued a brief release saying a non-nuclear bomb had been dropped and exploded in midair above the ocean before the crew bailed out. In subsequent interviews, surviving crew members said the bomb's plutonium core was not aboard the airplane.

That is where the story might have remained, except that three years later, in the summer of 1953, a rescue team searching the mountains of British Columbia for a lost civilian plane came across the wreck of the B-36. The strange thing was, the wreck was 300 miles north—back toward Alaska—rather than near the spot where the crew bailed out, when the plane, on autopilot and disabled, was heading down and south.

The 2000 article in the *Edmonton Journal* said that discovery led some to "maintain the bomb or its radioactive components, and perhaps a second nuclear weapon, remained on board the B-36 and that a lone crew member desperately tried to pilot the plane to safety, only to crash into a mountaintop in the province's remote interior."

Shortly after the wreck was discovered the American military descended on the crash site. They had a Geiger counter—which some said indicated they must have suspected radioactive material in the area—and explosives, which they used to obliterate the wreckage once they were finished with it. When they left, the Edmonton paper noted, "Rumors began circulating locally that a body had been recovered from the plane."

Surrounded by Reality

The *Edmonton Journal* did not speculate which crew member that might have been. But in an interview this week with the Canadian Press—the country's national newswire—filmmaker Michael Jorgensen says a team of experts, led by Canadian nuclear weapons researcher Dr. John Clearwater, believe one member of the crew did stay aboard the disabled plane and try to fly it back to Alaska.

"And that guy," Jorgensen said, "is the weaponeer—the guy responsible for the bomb, Captain Ted Schreier."

Jorgensen told the Canadian Press that he regards Schreier as a "hero" who "did everything in his power to try to save the weapon," which might have fallen into enemy hands had it been dumped into the Pacific. The filmmaker adds that something called a "birdcage"—an object used to transport the bomb's plutonium core, which is kept separate from the bomb—was found at the British Columbia crash site.

The surviving crew members—now there are only four—have always maintained there was no plutonium core aboard. Jorgensen interviewed two of them, and the filmmaker recalled, "The couple of guys that I interviewed . . . say, 'There are things that happened that we just can't talk about because we don't want to say anything to damage our country.'"

Jorgensen's conclusion: "I think there was a plutonium core in that birdcage. . . . I think it was on the mountain and I think it was taken out in 1954, when the Air Force went in there to destroy the airplane. It's my belief, given the evidence that we have, that a nuclear weapon laid in the mountains of northern Canada for four years."

Jorgensen told the Canadian Press that Schreier's family knew nothing of any of this. He reached Ted's nephew while shooting the documentary. "They were told when Ted went missing that he was on a transport plane," Jorgensen said. "They were totally shocked."

There was one other oddity, Jorgensen said. The Air

Force named streets after four of the five crew members who died in the crash of the B-36. The only one not getting the honor was Ted Schreier.

Friday, November 19, 2004

Steve Caravello, A Madison Great

Steve Caravello and Jack Nicklaus were walking down the ninth fairway at Odana Hills one summer day in 1962 when Nicklaus, the greatest player ever, put his arm around Caravello, the greatest Madison amateur golfer ever, and asked why Steve had never played the pro tour.

This was an exhibition, and Caravello was on his way to shooting 72 to Nicklaus' 70. Steve was telling me this story in June 2000. I had called him after watching Tiger Woods win the U.S. Open at Pebble Beach by 15 shots. We got onto other things, and his round with Nicklaus came up.

"Well," I remember saying, "why didn't you try the tour?"

"I couldn't find a backer," Caravello said. "I figured it would cost about $9,000 in those days, and I didn't have it."

He had the game. Caravello, who died here Thursday at 87, did some things on Midwest golf courses that may never be equaled. He won an incredible nine Madison men's city championships. He won back-to-back state amateur championships in 1956 and '57. He won the Tri-State Tournament held annually in Dubuque, Iowa, seven times; the Nakoma club championship 15 times. His course record 61 at Dubuque's Bunker Hill Country Club in the Tri-State still stands.

Surrounded by Reality

He was a natural in a sport that does not produce many of them, maybe because the golf swing is such an unnatural move. The club fit perfectly in his hands. His swing, seemingly effortless, launched rockets. As a kid, I would go to the tournaments and marvel at the ease with which he played.

Decades later, one of the many nice things that came out of my writing a book on the late columnist Mike Royko was that my son, Quinn, who is a good junior golfer, was able to spend a fair amount of time with Steve.

Steve's daughter Geri had married Mike's only brother, Bob Royko, and in getting to know the Roykos, I got to know Steve. There was so much more to him than golf. He was from an era when male friendship meant rough humor and road trips and practical jokes. Steve loved to tell stories about those days, about the time when he told his friend Harry Simonson that you could tell a "mature" ear of corn because it had exactly 364 kernels. A day or two later, in Simonson's house, he found three ears of corn covered with ballpoint pen marks. Harry had tried to count the kernels, and if you think Steve ever let him forget it, you're mistaken.

Another time Caravello was nearby at Nakoma when a foursome that included his good friend George Schiro drove into a blind fairway. Caravello ran out, scooped up all four balls—great drives—and ran off. The next day in the club bar Schiro began telling him the story: "We don't know what could have happened." Caravello reached into his pocket. "Recognize these?"

He and Schiro and a couple of guys were on a northern fishing trip once when one of their buddies set an alarm for 5 a.m. and went to sleep. It was midnight. Steve promptly set all the clocks and watches ahead five hours, and the alarm duly rang. Everyone hopped up, got in the boats, and after an hour and a half the guy who set the alarm was screaming in his boat: "Something's wrong! It's not getting light today!" He didn't realize it was 1:30 in the

162

morning. That was so good Mike Royko got a column out of it.

Madison attorney Tim Sweeney tells of caddying for Caravello at Nakoma (Steve himself got his start in golf caddying for George Vitense at Glenway). As Sweeney tells it, Steve was putting on the ninth green at Nakoma when a crow started bothering him. "I'm standing to the side holding his clubs," Sweeney said. "He's about to putt, and a crow starts squawking. Steve glares at the crow, and it stops. He starts to putt, and the crow squawks again. Steve walks over to me, unzips the bag, takes out a pistol, and shoots the crow!"

His best role may have been as patriarch to a family that is as loving as any I have been privileged to be near. Steve and his wife, Ann, raised four daughters, and now there are grandchildren and great-grandchildren, and to be at Bob and Geri Royko's house for the annual family gathering on Christmas Eve is to be overwhelmed by the warmth and humor and love they share. Not to mention the food. Around them you eat like kings. I recall Catherine Murray once writing that the pepper stuffed with roast beef that Steve and Ann served at the Italian restaurant they ran for a time on the east side "brought new heights to the stuffed pepper. I shall never forget it." That may be the most lyrical thing ever written about a stuffed pepper.

Steve was too ill to golf near the end—he got his competitive fix playing cards—but he shot his age into his 80s, and one day in 2002 he played a few holes at Maple Bluff with my son.

I cherish that memory. Watching him, I remember thinking of what another writer once said of another athlete. It seemed appropriate to recall it thinking of Steve's magical golf swing, and it seemed particularly appropriate for Thursday. He said that when you see anything at all done so perfectly well, you don't cheer. You cry.

Tuesday, November 23, 2004

Stray Ends Up with Royal Treatment

Just how a wonderfully friendly stray dog, Maggie, whose ancestors cavorted with Caribbean pirates, recently left O'Hare airport in the backseat of a limousine is a tale worth exploring.

If there is a moral to the story, it just may be that sometimes in this world, it is better to be a dog than a human being. Especially if you are trying to catch an airplane.

It all started because a well-known Madison couple, Todd and Liz Tiefenthaler, who own Kramer Printing, fell in love with the small, quiet island of Anguilla in the British West Indies.

The Tiefenthalers liked it so much they decided to do a book about the island, which is a little less daunting an undertaking when you own a printing company.

The book, *Anguilla: A Shorter Sleeved Way of Life,* should be available early next year.

On October 30, with the book in the final production process and a laser proof in hand, the Tiefenthalers headed for Anguilla one more time to fact-check and get some buzz going with the Anguillan tourism authorities. Another couple, Steve Stanczyk and Angela Baldwin-Stanczyk, accompanied them. Steve, who is Kramer's senior art director, designed the new book.

The trip was a success—the book was well received—and the group had ample opportunity to kick back with their toes in the sand, which is the national pastime of Anguilla.

The Best of Doug Moe on Madison

It was during one of those grueling beachside afternoons that Liz and Angela noticed the dog. It is probably worth noting parenthetically that I have never known a woman who could resist a dog. It's largely true of men, too, but it's more true of women, and Liz and Angela did not disappoint.

Of course they didn't. Noticing that the dog, which had crawled into the shade under their beach chairs, was a little thin, they bought it a sandwich at the snack bar.

It turned out the dog was a member of an unofficial breed known in the Caribbean as an Anguillan long dog. Originally brought to the island by pirates, the dogs' distinguishing characteristic is that they are long.

The women called the dog Maggie, and it developed that Maggie was little more than a puppy as well as a stray—dependent, like Blanche DuBois, on the kindness of strangers.

Naturally, the women fed the dog all week, every time they saw it, which was often. Maggie ate better than King Farouk.

Eventually, of course, the day of departure loomed. You may not be surprised to learn that a phone call was placed to American Airlines: What is involved with bringing a dog from Anguilla to the United States?

It wasn't impossible. There were shots and paperwork required, but a trip to the vet on Anguilla could handle it. Steve and Angela had decided to adopt the dog. The final decision was made after midnight on November 6, the day of their early afternoon departure. Unfortunately, at sunrise, the dog wasn't there.

"It was the first time all week she wasn't on the beach," Steve was recalling Monday. He and Angela walked down the beach, feeling terrible. "Then we saw this black speck in the distance," Steve said.

It was Maggie. They got her to the vet, got the shots and paperwork handled, and caught a boat ride to St. Martin for their flight home. Forty-five minutes prior to departure, Steve gave Maggie a mild sedative and put her in the crate in which she would fly. "It was amazing how smoothly it had gone," Steve said.

The 757 jet was full. And just as the flight attendants were doing their final preparations for takeoff, a voice came over the loudspeaker: "Will Stephen Steinbeck report to the front of the plane?" Steve figured they were looking for him and had butchered his name.

At the front of the plane, a flight attendant said, "Your dog has escaped!"

Maggie had last been seen racing across the tarmac to the other side of the airport. The flight attendant ushered Steve down the stairs to a waiting golf cart. Several runways over, Maggie was sniffing some other dogs that were outside a chain link fence. A security truck pulled in next to their golf cart.

Steve got Maggie, and they told him to get in the security truck. It would be faster than the golf cart. But they couldn't move. Planes were landing on the runways between. They had to wait out three landings. "I was convinced my plane had left," Steve said. "With my passport, my luggage, my ticket, and my wife."

Instead, inside his plane, the pilot was doing a play-by-play for the passengers. "Angela told me he said, 'He has the dog!' and everyone cheered."

Twenty minutes had passed, but Steve got back to his plane, and Maggie went back in the crate. "I have no idea how she got out," he said. Everyone in the plane had a high five for Steve. At their subsequent stops, in San Juan and then Chicago, airport personnel asked about the dog. Word had gone out. Maggie was a celebrity.

Landing at O'Hare, Todd Tiefenthaler decided a limousine was the only proper way to transport the formerly homeless dog from Chicago to Madison. Today Maggie is adjusting well. Angela bought her a coat for the cold weather.

The story is already a legend in Anguilla. Steve has the e-mails to prove it.

"I know one thing," he said. "They never would have held that plane for a person."

=====

Early Pilot Recalls Highs of Flying

On June 23, 1945, on a little strip of grass between two rows of trees outside of Shawano, Wisconsin, a J-3 Piper Cub airplane lifted slowly off the ground.

The pilot was a 30-year-old Green Bay native, Pauline Clough, and as the small plane climbed into the sky she let out a holler.

"You're up here all alone!"

On Tuesday, Clough, 90, sat on a sofa in her apartment on Madison's near west side and held an aged pilot's logbook in her hands. She pointed to a date on a line that said, "First solo flight." Her blue eyes sparkled. "It was so exciting," she said. "It's exciting now, just remembering."

Clough made between 250 and 300 flights in an era when women pilots were considerably rarer than they are today, and even now they are not exactly plentiful—6 percent of all licensed pilots, by one informed estimate.

There were maybe 100 female pilots in the whole country when Clough decided she would one day learn to fly. Some kids fall in love with baseball or the movies—for her it was airplanes. This was the mid-1920s and she was not quite a teenager. Every spare minute she spent at Green Bay's small airport.

"I would ride my bike out there every weekend," she said. "I talked about airplanes and flying to anyone who would talk to me. Every so often, somebody would say, 'I have to fly to Milwaukee. Would you like to come along?' They'd check with my mom and dad, and I'd get to go."

Pauline married James Clough—"It's English, and rhymes with rough and tough," she said with a smile—in 1937 and they moved to Shawano. Her childhood infatuation with flying never really went away, but by 1940 she had a baby and a job outside the home. Money was a concern, private air flight a distant luxury. Distant, except that Pauline soon got a job in the office of the Farmers Brewery, a small beer maker that had a German brew master, Kurt Guida, who had been a pilot in World War I and who retained a keen interest in flying.

"He was on a civil aeronautics board and would have people in to talk about flying," Clough said. "My office was the only warm place in the brewery, so they'd sit there. I remember telling them, 'Someday, I will fly.' "

One day in February 1945, Guida, who ran the brewery, said to Pauline, "As soon as you get the bank deposit ready, I want you to drive to the airport and ask for Red Leatherby."

The Shawano "airport" consisted of a small building on the edge of a tree-lined field that served as the runway. Clough introduced herself to Leatherby, a large, friendly man with fiery red hair.

"Are you ready to go?" Leatherby asked.

Guida had arranged, and paid for, a flying lesson.

"I was dumbfounded," Clough said. "I never expected it."

The date was February 26, 1945. Leatherby was the instructor. "I'm sure he took off for us," Clough said, but she had a turn at the controls and was completely hooked, as she had known she would be. "I do not like roller coasters," she said. "But I loved to fly."

She began taking weekly lessons from Leatherby.

"I didn't tell my husband," she said. "I was afraid he'd say we couldn't afford to spend the money."

The lessons were $8 an hour.

Into April and May, she began taking two and three lessons a week.

"What about your job?"

"They could make beer without me," she said Tuesday, chuckling.

She eventually told her husband, of course, and he didn't blink. There was only one other woman in the area taking lessons, and Clough doesn't know whether she ever got a license. Clough's first solo flight, in June 1945, was a milestone although she still didn't have a license, which would have allowed her to take passengers.

In January 1946, she bought an airplane, an Aeronca, for under $2,000, and there were weeks when she flew almost every day. Takeoff was over beautiful Shawano Lake, and there were moments in that plane alone when she had never felt such elation or serenity.

In September 1946, at the airport in Fond du Lac, she took her first test for the license that would allow her to take passengers. It was windy; she bounced on landing, and didn't pass. "I cried," she said.

She had lessons every day for a week, took the test again, and passed. She called her mom in Green Bay, who had never been in an airplane in her life, and asked if she wanted to be her daughter's first passenger. Her mom said yes and Pauline picked her up in Green Bay that afternoon.

Late in 1948, Pauline's husband was laid off and they decided to buy a tavern, which necessitated her selling her airplane. "I hated to give it up," she said. "But we needed the money." There were two sons by then, and eventually the family moved to Madison. One of her sons became a pilot and bought a plane, but Pauline never flew as a pilot again.

She has her pilot's log and her memories, and this

week, when someone asked if she had ever had a close call as a pilot, she said, "Just one time. Landing at Sturgeon Bay when it was about 10 degrees and my propeller stopped."

Stopped? "The engine quit!"

"What did you do?"

"I think I prayed a little," Pauline Clough said, "and I just coasted in."

She smiled. "It was a real good landing."

═══════════

Saturday, December 25, 2004

A Salute to Grit and Perseverance

Talking about his dad this week, Gannon Boyd said, "He would have loved all this."

Boyd is an account executive with a high-tech company in Santa Barbara, California. His dad, Jerry Boyd, had a history of heart problems, and died in 2002 at age 72. But this is about how he lived, not died, and it was quite a life. Now Clint Eastwood is playing Boyd in a movie, roughly speaking, and of course Jerry would have loved it.

For all the grit and color that surrounded his life, Boyd was not, by the time he reached age 70, a success in any conventional sense.

"I failed at everything," he told the *New York Times* in August 2000. "I failed with every woman, I failed as a father, I failed as a writer. I was a bullfighter, but I wasn't good enough to be a matador. I wrote, but I wasn't a writer."

His dad was an immigrant from Ireland. Jerry was born in Long Beach and raised in Gardena, south of Los Angeles. Before he was out of Gardena High School, he was shining shoes in gambling clubs. There was a softer side courtesy of his mother, who taught him to bake pies. He was acting, too, first in high school and then at Los Angeles City College, which he left in 1951 with a drama degree.

It was the acting, particularly after a stint studying nights under Sanford Meisner at the Neighborhood Playhouse in New York City (where he had been shipped by the Navy Reserves), that led Boyd to begin writing. Plays, none produced. He'd read Hemingway, of course, so there was the obligatory pilgrimage to Spain and, later, an actual run as a bullfighter in Mexico, where he was gored several times. Doubtless the three women who married and eventually divorced him realized this was a man unconsumed by the need for a mortgage and a savings plan.

Winding up back in Los Angeles, no longer a young man, he bartended to support his writing habit. "I'd submit things and I'd be destroyed when they were rejected," Boyd told the *New York Times*. "But then I'd crawl back to the typewriter and do some more. This went on for years and years, and it hurt so bad."

There was another, somewhat latent passion— unlikely, in that boxing is a young man's game. By the time Boyd found the gyms, he had lived nearly half a century. "In my mid and late 40s, I came to boxing by choice and by chance," he would write later. He fought until he really was too old for that, and then he worked as a trainer and a cut man, the guy in a boxer's corner who stops the bleeding when a wound is opened in the ring. In the grunts and sweat of the sweet science, Jerry Boyd found the magic to make his writing come alive.

"I stop blood," is how Boyd began one short story. He called it "The Monkey Look" and sent it out to a small magazine in California, which printed it. Somehow a New York literary agent spotted it, got hold of the author, and asked if he'd written anything else.

The author was calling himself F.X. Toole, because he

really didn't want his pals at the gym to know about his other vocation. Toole sent the agent some more of his writing, the agent sent it to an editor in New York, Daniel Halpern, who read it in October 1999 on his commute home from Manhattan to New Jersey. By the time the train reached Princeton, Halpern knew he would publish this extraordinary collection of boxing stories, titled *Rope Burns*.

The book came out the following summer. Boyd was 70. The reviews were splendid. "He went on a book tour to Ireland," Boyd's son, Gannon, told me when we spoke this week. "My grandfather was from there, and my dad got to see the family home."

There was talk of a movie, options, this or that actor was interested. It didn't happen when Jerry was alive. "He had a triple bypass when I was in college," Gannon said, "in the early 1990s." Increasingly, there were hospital visits, shortness of breath, angioplasties. He died in a hospital in Torrance.

At some point Clint Eastwood got interested in the project, and that changed everything. Still, even with Eastwood's clout, the financing was hard. A pitch for a dark movie about boxing seemed guaranteed to leave a studio executive staring blankly into the middle distance.

But Eastwood got it made, starring, directing, even composing the score. The early reviews of *Million Dollar Baby*—based on a blend of two of the stories in *Rope Burns*—have been rapturous. The movie will open in Madison next month.

Gannon Boyd has seen it, of course, and pronounced it wonderful. He told me there is a plan to reissue the book next month; and a novel, almost completed by his dad before his death, may be published later in 2005.

So here's to Jerry Boyd, and to all the other scarred and beautiful fools, the busted valises, who somehow find the courage to keep dreaming. Here's to F.X. Toole.

Merry Christmas, everybody.

Monday, December 27, 2004

Another Christmas in Jail Cell

As the sun went down a week ago today, an Ohio attorney, Farhad Sethna, sent out an e-mail expressing the hope that his client, Ashraf Al-Jailani, would be home for Christmas.

"Some good breaking news this Christmas season," Sethna wrote.

It was not that good, as it turned out. Al-Jailani spent Christmas in a jail cell, where he has been since October 2002.

He has not been charged with a crime.

This man's treatment at the hands of the government of the United States has been despicable. No less a word will do.

I first wrote about it in October 2003—a year after Al-Jailani had been led from his job in handcuffs—because a judge had finally ordered the government to produce at least some evidence as to why it was holding a man without bond or the filing of charges.

At that hearing, a portion of the "evidence" against Al-Jailani was a Wisconsin identification card that showed him with an east side Madison address. That same apartment building, the government claimed, had been home to a mysterious figure identified only as "Suspect B," a suspected international terrorist. That ID card, along with some phone call records from Al-Jailani's home to a New York number linked to terrorists, convinced the government that Al-Jailani, Yemen-born and married to an American, was a deadly terrorist—an al-Qaida "first-stringer, highly educated, highly

173

trained and highly motivated," according to the FBI agent who testified at the hearing.

I figured that if an apartment on Madison's east side had housed a top al-Qaida terrorism cell, that constituted news, and somebody here should write about it. After all, this "Suspect B" might still be running around the east side.

Unfortunately, when I contacted federal law enforcement officials both here and in Ohio, they declined to discuss the case.

Al-Jailani's wife, Michele Swensen, whom he had met when both were in college in Japan, explained to me how he happened to have the ID with a Madison address. They had moved to the United States, to Swensen's native Ohio, and got married.

"It was 1996," Swensen said. "He had just come to the United States. He was checking out geology graduate programs and had heard that Madison's was good. He stayed only a couple of months. . . . He was new to America and had no driver's license, so his friend in Madison told him to get an ID card, that it was easy. So that's what Ashraf did, and that's why he had an ID card from Madison. He had no idea that years later, that ID card would cause him so much trouble."

Though Al-Jailani and "Suspect B" had the same Madison apartment building as an address, further investigation showed they did not live in the same apartment unit.

Two months after the hearing in which the government claimed Al-Jailani was a first-string international terrorist, the Ohio judge who presided, Walt Durling, issued an 11-page ruling ridiculing the government's case. "If one steps back a moment and examines the government's theory," Durling wrote, "there is no direct evidence linking respondent to terrorism, only certain indirect links to others known or suspected of being associated with terrorism."

The hearing also revealed that the government had

not even bothered to question Al-Jailani during the entire first year it had him in custody. His attorney, Sethna, filed a Freedom of Information Act request with the FBI to see its files on Al-Jailani. "I got one page saying there were no files," Sethna said.

Still, the Department of Homeland Security appealed Judge Durling's ruling that Al-Jailani be permitted bail. Al-Jailani continued to sit in jail.

Then, this past summer, with Al-Jailani approaching two years of incarceration, the government got even nastier. Stymied in its effort to convince anyone Al-Jailani is a terrorist, it suggested he should be deported back to Yemen because he is a threat to Swensen, his wife.

After a December 1998 argument in a mall parking lot in which Swensen's glasses were knocked from her face, Al-Jailani had been ordered deported, as even a misdemeanor domestic violence conviction is grounds for deportation under the 1996 Immigration Act. *New York Times* columnist Anthony Lewis wrote about the case, and Ohio governor Bob Taft pardoned Al-Jailani, saving him from deportation.

This summer, the government—having photocopied Swensen's electronic diary—resurrected the issue, saying Al-Jailani is currently a threat to Swensen. An appellate court agreed. Never mind that Swensen has fought for two years to try to free him. The *Akron Beacon Journal* editorialized, "It is an embarrassment that the government, its allegations of terrorism unsupported, is pressing for deportation on the grounds of domestic violence."

On December 17, after still more hearings and with Al-Jailani still in jail, a judge ruled that while he would not grant Al-Jailani asylum, neither would he order Al-Jailani deported to Yemen, lest he face recriminations there for the terrorism allegations made against him by the U.S. government. It was that ruling that led Sethna to say Al-Jailani could be released by Christmas. He wasn't—the

175

government has announced it is again appealing.

It is mind-boggling, as if there is no depth to which our government, in our employ, will not sink. In one hearing in November, when Al-Jailani's lawyer first mentioned Ashraf might be in danger if he was sent back to Yemen, a government lawyer actually suggested it was Al-Jailani's own fault that so many people know he was suspected of terrorism. Wasn't it his own wife and lawyer who have been talking to the media?

That is the government's logic. If only Al-Jailani had sat quietly in his cell for 26 months, not having been questioned, not having been charged, if only he had sat just there in the dark, his supporters saying nothing, then everything would be OK.

2005

===

A High-Flying Life Comes to End

When Lieutenant Gene Welch came home to Madison on leave from the Air Force in April 1944, he'd already flown 25 combat missions over Germany and France and been credited with shooting down at least 11 Nazi planes.

Welch, a Madison native and East High grad who died last month at 87, came home with a distinguished flying cross, the Air Medal with three oak leaf clusters, and an air ticket for California. After three weeks in Madison, Welch flew to the west coast, where the Air Force put him up at the Shangri-La hotel in Santa Monica while he underwent physicals and a debriefing.

The hotel looked out on the ocean, and there was enough down time for Welch to call a friend in Culver City. They spent a day together, and that evening the friend drove Welch back to his hotel in a red roadster. As Welch got out of the car, a woman coming from the Shangri-La said, "Your friend sure looks like Clark Gable."

Surrounded by Reality

It was Gable, all right. The *Gone With the Wind* star and Welch had met a year earlier in Polebrook, England, when Gable was assigned to Welch's 351st Bomb Group. That day in California, Gable introduced Welch to Fred Astaire on the lot at MGM. Astaire was shooting a scene from *Ziegfeld Follies* with Lucille Ball, but he wanted to talk to Welch, since Welch and Astaire's sister, Adele, had been friends in London and were together the night of February 23, when London suffered its worst blitz since 1940.

"I had a long talk with him about his sister and England," Welch recalled later in a letter home to Madison. Astaire, he said, was smaller than he thought, but had large hands.

"Your friend Gable got me into pictures," Astaire told Welch. "It was *Dancing Lady*, and I played myself."

There were those in Madison who thought Gene Welch ought to be up there on the big screen himself. He had that kind of life. And while Welch never made it into a movie himself, he shot a scene that did, a sequence from his fighter plane that Gable included in his documentary, *Combat America*.

Welch grew up on the near east side, Spaight Street, graduating from East in 1935 and getting a bachelor of science degree at UW–Madison in 1939. The wildness of spirit that was Welch's calling card was evidenced early, according to his East High classmate, Madison baseball legend Ernie Bruns.

"He was one colorful character," Bruns was saying Tuesday. "I remember him driving down Langdon Street in a red convertible, standing up while he drove!"

Welch attended law school in Madison for a couple of years, but he ached to be a fighter ace. In 1941, prior to the United States entering World War II, Welch crossed the border to Canada. In November 1942 he received his wings in the Royal Canadian Air Force, graduating as a bomber pilot in Alberta.

By the following month Welch was in England. In April 1942 he transferred into the U.S. Air Force and began flying the famous B-17 Flying Fortress in missions over continental Europe. There was at least one close call after a raid on Nantes in occupied France, when Welch's plane took more than 300 flak and bullet holes and lost two engines because the gas supply ran out. Welch was able to coast the huge plane to an emergency landing on the English coast.

Gable showed up at Welch's base in England in 1943. They became friends, spent a leave in London together, and Welch took a camera up in his plane to shoot footage that Gable could use in the documentary he was making.

When the two met up in southern California a year later—the day that Gable introduced Welch to Astaire—the star offered to screen the as-yet-unreleased documentary for Welch. "I spotted the scene I'd taken of an enemy plane blowing up," Welch wrote home to Madison. "Gable asked me how I liked it, and I feel both he and the boys that helped him film it did a great job to let the American people know just what a job their boys are doing."

After the war, Welch stayed here in Madison for a time with the Air Force, which allowed him to teach as an assistant professor in aeronautics at the department of air sciences. It was, one might guess, a bit tame for Gene Welch. In any case he was soon gone to the Azores, where he served as assistant operations officer at the Air Force's transport station. It was not a desk job. Welch flew planes and helicopters and made a number of sea rescues of marooned boaters. In 1957, he took the first pictures of a new island created by an incredible volcano off the coast of Faial in the Azores. The flames shot 200 feet high, the smoke 16,000 feet.

In 1974, perhaps ready at last for a bit of calm, Welch took a teaching position at a college in Savannah, Georgia. It was in a Savannah hospital that Welch died December 22. His old friend, Ernie Bruns, said Welch got back to Madison frequently, most recently to their 60th East High reunion in 1995. "He was all over the room that night," Bruns said. "Just like always."

There was a moment during that day in California with Gable when an actress came up to Welch during a break. She was a beautiful redhead who rode a white horse on the merry-go-round in *Ziegfeld Follies*. She'd heard Welch was a war hero and wanted to know what it was like to be shot at. They all had lunch at the MGM cafeteria, and at one point you could hear somebody at the next table say, "Who's that kid with Gable?"

"Some nobody," Welch said.

Gable winked. "Don't you believe it," he said.

Friday, January 14, 2005

Hot Dog!
Oscar Ode Still Lives

Sunday's edition of the *Boston Globe* included a story on the demise of the jingle—the cheerful tunes used to sell products on radio and television.

The *Globe* quoted a prominent advertising executive saying, "The jingle is dead."

The culprit is an evolving marketplace where mood-producing pop songs are preferred over original jingles. The jingle "is too quaint, too corny, too old school for our ironic times," the paper notes. "Naming your product in a commercial for your product is just tacky."

But the *Globe* also said this: "Of course, there are exceptions. The Oscar Mayer wiener theme has been in constant rotation since 1963, and good money says everyone reading this newspaper can sing it start to finish."

Richard Trentlage knows it. He knows the tune and he knows it is still being played. Of course he does. Just the other day the mailman brought him a royalty check for $2,728.65.

Trentlage wrote the Oscar Mayer wiener jingle.

All together now:

"Oh, I wish I were an Oscar Mayer wiener

"That is what I'd truly like to be

"Cause if I were an Oscar Mayer wiener

"Everyone would be in love with me!"

"The gem of my writing career," Trentlage was saying Thursday. He is 76 and lives outside of Chicago in Fox River Grove.

The jingle has aired on radio and TV in 19 countries and been performed by some of the world's great symphonies. So venerable is the Oscar Mayer wiener jingle that in 1998 Trentlage thought it should be in the *Guinness Book of World Records* as the longest-running advertising jingle ever. "You have to research it," Trentlage said of the *Guinness* honor. "They don't just take your word for it." Finally a librarian was located in New York City who was the acknowledged expert on such matters. Alas, Trentlage's Oscar Mayer jingle ran second.

"Chiquita Banana beat us by 20 years," he said.

Still, you need to go back to the early 1960s for the genesis of the wiener song. Oscar G. Mayer, son of founder Oscar F. Mayer, was running the company in Madison. The company's advertising agency, J. Walter Thompson in Chicago, was told to find a jingle that would sell hot dogs. The agency decided to sponsor a contest inviting people to compose a jingle—on spec, no money up front—for Oscar Mayer wieners.

Trentlage, at the time, was working for another agency in Chicago, but he had branched out on his own writing jingles, with considerable success. A friend heard about the Oscar Mayer contest and called Trentlage, saying it was right up his alley. Trentlage had worked as a butcher's boy as a kid. The only hitch was the contest deadline was the next day.

That evening at home, Trentlage put a sheet of paper in the typewriter. He knew it had to be short, and appeal to moms and kids. "I wrote 10 ideas down, like I always do," Trentlage said. "That gets rid of the crap. Then I wrote 10 more ideas down."

Eventually he wrote, "Oh, I wish I were an Oscar Mayer wiener."

He recalled, "Then I thought, Why? Why do I wish I were an Oscar Mayer wiener?"

He typed, "Because everyone would be in love with me."

He scratched here and there, added a bit, and when he had something he was happy with he gathered his son and daughter, 10 and 9 respectively at the time, and got them on tape singing the jingle.

"The next morning," Trentlage said, "I went to the J. Walter Thompson office, right when they opened, found the correct desk, and put the tape on it. Remember, I'm working at a competing agency at the time. I wasn't to be seen there."

And then . . . nothing. For a year, Trentlage heard not a word. But there came a day in 1963 when he picked up his phone and somebody was giving him congratulations. He heard later that Thompson had received 203 entries and had matched them against one another in brackets, in a kind of a wiener-jingle NCAA basketball tournament.

With Trentlage's tape in hand, the J. Walter Thompson executives drove to up to Madison. Oscar G. Mayer himself was running the meeting. The tape was played and everyone looked to the head of the table.

"It's wonderful," Mayer said. "You made that little girl

sound like she has a cold. Every mother has a daughter who has sounded like that!"

On Thursday, Trentlage chuckled. "My daughter had a stuffy nose the night we recorded it."

Sent out to radio stations, it was an immediate sensation. "It sold hot dogs so fast they couldn't believe it," Trentlage said. Station music directors were stunned when listeners began calling up and requesting it like a hit song. All this did not make the Trentlage family poor. "My kids had college paid for while they were still in elementary school," he said.

Trentlage kept writing jingles—somewhere between 600 and 800, he estimates—and had other successes, though nothing to match his ode to the wiener. While he appreciates the humor of it, Trentlage is proud of his craft. He's writing a book he has titled, *So You Want to Be a Jingle Writer.*

"It's a lot more than rhyming *June* and *moon,*" he said. "You need a sales-oriented line that will move the goods."

Trentlage may not know this, but on Thursday, a check of the Chiquita website revealed that in 1999, a year after his *Guinness* search, the banana company changed the lyrics of its jingle—to "highlight the nutrition benefits," the company said.

Since their original jingle is no longer running, you could argue that, sometime in 2019, the Oscar Mayer wiener jingle (56 years) may pass the first Chiquita banana jingle (55 years) as the longest continuously running jingle in the world. So Richard Trentlage may yet find himself in the *Guinness* book, embraced by history, everyone loving him, as they do the wiener he immortalized.

Will the jingle be playing in 2019? Before you answer, try getting it out of your head right now.

Tuesday, January 25, 2005

Onion Guy Comes Well Disguised

Steve Hannah was walking through an airport the other day wearing his *Onion* baseball cap when a young guy grabbed him and demanded to know where he got the lid.

"Don't I look like an *Onion* guy?" Hannah said.

"Well, no."

"*Onion* guys come in all shapes and sizes," Hannah said.

Onion guy, newspaper guy, budding business tycoon, no matter—what does matter is that at the moment Steve Hannah is having more fun than you, me, and most everybody else.

Worse, he's calling it work.

For the past year, Hannah, 55, has been running *The Onion*, serving as chief executive officer of the hip humor weekly that started in Madison on less than a shoestring in 1988. Today it's a multimedia juggernaut with a world-famous website, print editions in cities across the country, a syndicated radio deal, best-selling books, and a movie set for release later this year.

Hannah—perhaps best remembered as a reporter and then an editor at the *Milwaukee Journal*—was here Monday to address the Madison Advertising Federation on all things *Onion*. He showed up for the noon luncheon at the Sheraton looking classy-casual in sport coat, blue jeans, loafers, and—of course—his *Onion* cap. He charmed the crowd—the group's largest in three years—by tossing off *Onion* headlines and insider anecdotes that occasionally employed words of less than five and more than three letters. Racy is better if it's funny, and the ad crowd is not precisely polite company. Hannah seemed in a good mood and it was contagious.

Aging news hounds do not, as a rule, grab the brass ring. For every obit writer who comes out of nowhere with a great American novel there are a thousand others bitter that Maxwell Perkins died without discovering them.

Certainly they are not supposed to understand commerce or make any real money.

Hannah began earning his financial chops even before escaping the newspaper business. He became managing editor of the *Milwaukee Journal,* a position as much about business as bylines, leaving around the time of the paper's merger with the *Sentinel.* Hannah began a weekly syndicated column and a public relations business that landed a big Wisconsin financial concern, Strong Funds, as its flagship client.

Working with the New York-based financial press took Hannah to Manhattan often, and there he eventually formed a good friendship with David Schafer, who owns Schafer Capital Management.

A few years ago, Hannah took a phone call from another good friend, Madison attorney Brady Williamson, whose firm represents *The Onion.*

"*The Onion* needs an angel," Williamson said.

Though the paper had moved to New York City and its profile had never been higher, the bottom line was less exciting. Bottom line? It had always been more fun to write headlines than save receipts. Now costs were escalating and new projects were being put on hold and something had to be done.

"They were undercapitalized," Hannah was saying Monday.

After speaking to Williamson, Hannah phoned Schafer, the New York financial guru. "Have you heard of *The Onion*?" Hannah said. Schafer knew the paper because his son was going to school in Boulder, Colorado, a big *Onion* town. Hannah continued, "*The Onion* needs someone with deep pockets who won't get in the way."

Schafer was the guy. "David bought a majority interest," Hannah said. And while he didn't get in the way in any creative sense, Schafer did institute a few changes on the business side, suggesting, for instance, that perhaps there should be an annual budget. Now it's making money again and everyone's happy.

Hannah owns a piece, too, and he got drafted as CEO a year ago. "The idea was we needed somebody with gray hair to watch the children," he said, but he said it with a grin, and it is clear he has both respect and affection for *The Onion*'s ramshackle creative team. "I love the product," Hannah said.

What's not to love? It's cool and hip and Hannah knows it. How hip? The paper recently turned down a chance to have a regular presence on Jay Leno's *Tonight Show*. Not edgy enough.

When he took the job, his son said, "Dad, if you can't get kissed working for *The Onion*, you can't get kissed," though the younger Hannah did not say "kissed" and neither did Steve, telling the story Monday.

Now there is a movie and yet another book on the way, and soon, in an airport somewhere, a middle-aged former newspaper guy will once again be asked to explain how he got his cap.

Friday, February 4, 2005

How Many Lawyers Does It Take . . . ?

An incident in New York last month may require UW–Madison law professor Marc Galanter to revise his upcoming book, *Lowering the Bar: Lawyer Jokes and Legal Culture.*

Galanter has been working on the book for some time. I first interviewed him about it five years ago. I wasn't able to reach him Thursday to see how he's progressing, but a legal trade publication, *Voir Dire,* had a piece on Galanter and his book last spring saying the book is "forthcoming."

I hope it's not in type yet. This New York episode is worth including.

According to the Long Island newspaper *Newsday,* two men, Harvey Kash, 69, and Carl Lanzisera, 65, were arrested for telling lawyer jokes while waiting in line to get into First District Court in Nassau County.

"How can you tell when a lawyer is lying?" Kash asked in a loud voice.

"His lips are moving," Lanzisera replied.

"What's the difference between a vulture and a lawyer?"

"Wing tips."

"Why do they bury lawyers 100 feet into the ground?"

"Because deep down, they're good people."

Kash and Lanzisera are founders of Americans for Legal Reform, a group that among other things does not appreciate attorneys.

The two men were in fine voice that day last month,

but a few places ahead in line, someone called back, "Shut up! I'm a lawyer."

They did not. *Newsday* reported that the lawyer then reported them to courthouse personnel, who arrested them on charges of disorderly conduct. Lanzisera told the paper, "They put the handcuffs on us, brought us into a room, frisked us. . . . They were very, very nasty."

A Nassau courts spokesman said, "They were being abusive, and they were causing a disturbance."

If the incident does nothing else, it shows that emotions about the legal system still run high.

Back in 2000, Galanter told me his book would include around 350 lawyer jokes, along with the professor's scholarly take on what the jokes reveal in the context of both popular and legal culture.

Galanter thinks the nature of lawyer jokes changed about 25 years ago. Until 1980 or so, the jokes were usually linked to aspects of the profession and could be complimentary.

For instance: A guy is on trial for stealing a horse. His defense lawyer gives a great closing argument, and the guy is acquitted. Walking out of the courthouse, the lawyer says, "Did you steal the horse?" The guy says, "I thought I did until I heard your closing argument."

But then the jokes turned more vicious. What do you call 5,000 lawyers on the bottom of the sea? A good start. What's the difference between a skunk and a lawyer lying dead in the road? There are skid marks in front of the skunk.

Galanter thinks the shift in tone came with changes in society that didn't always have a lot to do with attorneys. An airline bumps you from a flight, or shorts you on frequent flier miles. Your HMO refuses to cover something. People are strangling on red tape and sometimes, of course, lawyers are involved. "People have this notion that there should be natural harmony in society," Galanter said. "Lawyers are locked in at just the spot where that doesn't hold."

The Best of Doug Moe on Madison

Out in New Jersey, the two men arrested for telling the jokes were immediately deluged with offers by lawyers to represent them, a circumstance that has the makings of a joke itself. They ended up choosing a prominent civil rights attorney, Ron Kuby, who has a radio show in New York City.

Last week, *Newsday* reported that Nassau prosecutors had dropped the charges against Lanzisera, but will proceed with the case against Kash, who is scheduled to appear before a grand jury Monday.

"I feel like public enemy number one," Kash said.

If Kash is overcome with the desire to tell a lawyer joke that day, let me suggest he go with one of what Marc Galanter called the "more cerebral" jokes. He might even utilize Galanter's favorite.

There's a rich old guy who, on his deathbed, isn't certain about the old adage you can't take it with you. He calls in his three closest advisers—a priest, a doctor and a lawyer—and gives them each $100,000 in an envelope. "Please drop them in my casket," the guy says. "Just in case."

The guy dies, and the three advisers each put an envelope in the casket before the burial. Later, they're talking, and the priest says, "I have to confess I kept $20,000 out for our homeless fund." The doctor says, "I'll admit I kept $50,000 for our AIDS fund. But I put the rest in."

The lawyer shakes his head. "Shame on the two of you."

The doctor says, "You mean you put it all in the casket?"

The lawyer smiles. "I put in my personal check for $100,000."

≡≡≡

Monday, February 14, 2005

"He's Had a Heart Attack"
Interview Subject Collapses at Home

I had come to talk about Leo Burt, Madison's most notorious fugitive, a suspect in the 1970 bombing on campus that took the life of a young researcher.

I ended up trying desperately to help save the life of the man I had come to see.

Some months ago I contracted to write a magazine article on Burt, perhaps the last of the Vietnam-era fugitives. The piece is scheduled to run this summer on the 35th anniversary of the bombing.

My deadline was looming, and this past Thursday I had an appointment for the last of my interviews.

Allan Thompson is retired from the Madison office of the Federal Bureau of Investigation. He was, for a long time, one of the lead investigators on the bombing case. He's an expert when it comes to tracking fugitives, and he found a lot of them. Leo Burt had frustrated him, as I learned when we first spoke, a decade ago, for an earlier article.

"I did fugitive work for 23 years," Thompson told me in 1995. "In every case I worked, someone in the woodwork knew where the person was. Family, friends—somebody. With Burt, there was an intense investigation of his parents and relatives. Nothing came of it. Not one iota in 25 years that he has been sighted, heard from, or spoken to."

Thursday morning, Thompson welcomed me into his home in Middleton. A tall, well-proportioned man in his late 60s, he asked if I wanted coffee and introduced me to his wife, Carol, who was friendly and gracious and said she would be going out soon.

She left as her husband and I began our interview, seated in the living room, facing each other. It proceeded well for several minutes and then Thompson stood and excused himself.

He was out of the room for two or three minutes. He came back, and I started to speak before sensing something was wrong.

Thompson had a strange look on his face. Suddenly he pitched forward, collapsing head first across a coffee table.

I cried out, "Mr. Thompson!"

I jumped from my seat. He was still sprawled across the table, his face flushed, his breath coming in short, harsh gasps.

I remember thinking, *Can this really be happening?*

I was unsure whether to move him, but then did, getting him off the table and onto his back on the floor.

I ran into the kitchen, where I had earlier seen Carol Thompson set down a mobile phone. I picked it up, walked toward the living room, and dialed 911.

The dispatcher, Middleton police sergeant Donald Mueller, answered immediately.

As best I can recall, I gave the address of the house, and then said, "A man has collapsed. I'm afraid he's had a heart attack."

I will say this for myself: I did not panic. I don't know if I did anything else right, but I didn't panic.

I recall that Mueller, the dispatcher—and I'm going from memory here and not a transcript—asked me a few questions. He was calm and I think that helped me stay calm. Could I feel a pulse? A heartbeat?

I replied that my own system was racing so fast that it was hard for me to tell. I said I thought I felt a pulse.

He said he was going to put me on hold for a moment

and call for the paramedics.

A few seconds later he was back. "Do you know CPR?"

"I don't," I said, mentally kicking myself. I had never bothered to learn because something like this might happen to other people, but never to me.

Mueller instructed me to tilt Thompson's head back, pinch his nostrils closed, and breathe into his mouth. I did that a few times and he seemed to breathe and sputter a bit. Mueller then had me apply pressure with my hands several times at the bottom of Thompson's ribcage.

It was then that Carol Thompson returned—she had forgotten her eyeglasses. Seeing me kneeling over her husband she let out a cry, but quickly calmed.

Mueller told me to ask Carol Thompson if her husband had any heart medicine. She was able to locate a nitroglycerin pill and place it under his tongue.

Mueller said, "They are outside the house right now."

Carol Thompson took over the mouth-to-mouth resuscitation and I ran to the door. The first one in was Middleton police officer Mark Walther. Right behind him was a neighbor of the Thompsons, Madison Fire Department paramedic Laura Graf. She had been heading out for a jog when she saw Walther's car and asked if she could help. Two Middleton paramedics, Ryan Kitterman and Jennifer Hort-Sandridge, were on the scene a short time later.

They all moved quickly and forcefully, clearing the table out of the way and ripping open Thompson's shirt. They spoke to Carol Thompson with a measured urgency, asking about allergies, medicines, and her husband's heart history.

I walked into the kitchen, put my hands on my knees and tried to compose myself.

From the kitchen I could see them hooking Thompson up to a defibrillator. Carol Thompson kept saying, "Don't leave me, Al." The medical team was voicing encouragement as well: "You can do it, Al."

This seems strange, but I recall the defibrillator speaking as well, giving computer-generated instructions.

What I remember most is the intensity and focus of the officers and paramedics as they did their jobs. I watched and in that moment I thought of an article my friend Bill Heinz wrote in the 1950s, for *Life* magazine, about a pioneering heart surgeon. Bill titled it, "The Man With a Life in His Hands."

But surgery, for all its pressures, is something for which a surgeon may prepare. Paramedics are dropped willy-nilly into life-and-death situations with many variables that require split-second decisions. They are special.

Now the paramedics had Thompson on a stretcher, and they were telling Carol Thompson that his heart was beating and he was breathing on his own. One called it "the best result after a cardiac arrest," but cautioned that they could not be sure of the extent of the damage that had been done.

Carol Thompson called me at home Thursday night. They were hopeful, she said, but he had not regained consciousness. They would know more in 24 hours.

Friday morning, a close friend of the Thompson family, retired Madison police officer George Croal, phoned me at the newspaper. "He woke up this morning," Croal said.

I closed my eyes and mouthed two words: Thank you.

Carol Thompson called me Friday afternoon. She said her husband, while groggy, was recognizing people, and doing fairly well, though he was not certain where he was or what had happened.

"He has no recollection of your visit," she said.

I thought to myself: *I remember*.

Sunday, a little past noon, I stopped by University Hospital. Carol Thompson told me with a smile that for the first time her husband knew where he was, and why. She

193

took me into his room and we shook hands. He was sitting up in a chair. He grinned and offered to start telling me about his investigation of Leo Burt.

Dan Cornett, the physician who had been caring for Thompson the past several days, stepped into the room. He had heard about his patient's progress but not seen him.

"Where are you?" Cornett asked.

"In a hospital in Madison, Wisconsin."

"Why are you here?"

"I had a heart attack."

The doctor smiled. "It's a miracle," he said.

═══════════

Thursday, February 24, 2005

"Last Show" for '50s-Style Dr. Bop

Mike Riegel, who under the name Dr. Bop was the founder and leader of one of the most popular bands ever to come out of Madison, died Monday in a Madison hospice. He was 60.

Dr. Bop and the Headliners, with Riegel on drums, shot to stardom in the early 1970s with a high-energy retro-'50s rock 'n' roll that proved irresistible to audiences wherever they went.

The first audiences were at the Nitty Gritty in Madison, where Marsh Shapiro gave them their start at $80 a week. Within months, managed by Ken Adamany, the band was playing college towns around the Midwest and the word was spreading. At its peak, the band played a six-night run at the Whiskey-a-Go-Go in Los Angeles and recorded a live album at Lucifer's in Boston. In September 1974, they played the Dane County Coliseum on a bill with the Eagles and Black Oak Arkansas.

"They were absolutely amazing," Adamany was recalling Wednesday. "Everybody had to have this band. You couldn't have a nightclub if you couldn't book Dr. Bop."

The band was born in a conversation between Riegel and Shapiro in 1971. Riegel was a Madison kid, a West High grad, the son of a prominent UW German professor, Sieghardt Riegel. Mike was studying art at UW–Madison— and he would become a fine painter—but he wanted to play music.

The Nitty Gritty was one of the few venues in those days, and one night Riegel asked Shapiro what he could play that Marsh wanted to hear.

"I sat him down at one of our picnic tables with five or six old 1950s straight rock 'n' roll albums," Shapiro said Wednesday.

In a 1978 interview, Riegel said he was less than overwhelmed with the idea. "At first it was embarrassing," he said. "We all thought of ourselves as serious musicians and were sure our reputations would be ruined. Entertaining was a foreign concept back then. Everyone took themselves so seriously, it was hard to loosen up."

Still, it was a gig. Riegel, Ken Champion, the guitarist, Larry Robertson, the keyboard player, and Ned Engelhart, the bass player, signed on to play the Gritty.

We went down to St. Vincent's," Riegel said, "and bought four used tuxedos and four pairs of shoes, which we sprayed with gold paint. . . . Then we went out and got bombed. I don't think we could have done it sober."

The Gritty crowd ate it up.

"The response we got was totally unexpected," Riegel said. "The audience just went crazy. We were getting encores and everything."

After the first few shows, Riegel felt their vocals were not up to the rest of the performance. He had a friend from the UW, Al Craven, who was teaching in New York but one weekend came to visit Riegel in Madison. Craven could sing, and once they got Craven inside the Nitty Gritty, and several beers inside Craven, he jumped onstage. "They gave me a tuxedo, and I started singing a Buddy Holly song," Craven was recalling Wednesday. The roars for Dr. Bop, already loud, became a crescendo.

"I started flying back every weekend," Craven said. "I did that for eight months."

Onstage, Craven was "The White Raven," and all the band members were given stage personas by Riegel, who of course was Dr. Bop, the band's heart and soul. An important early add was Bob Kenison, replacing Robertson on keyboards.

On Wednesday Kenison said, "There were a lot of '50s bands around at that time, but unlike many of them, we didn't spoof the music. We had fun, and Mike gave us our characters to play, but we respected the music."

Adamany concurs: "That's what separated them. They were really good musicians."

The original band broke up around 1978. Some members were weary of the travel and realized that hotel rooms do, in time, lose their romance. Riegel and Ned Engelhart kept the band going for the next 14 years, though, playing a variety of gigs in equally varied locales. "We had a roving party," is how Engelhart put it Wednesday. Some 42 people played in the band in its various incarnations. They were big in the Chicago area in the late '80s and early '90s.

"The Doctor decided to retire in 1992," Engelhart said, speaking of Riegel, though they came out of retirement in October 1993 to play the Nitty Gritty's 25th anniversary party.

Engelhart said his friend had finally tired of the road. In later years Riegel painted, told stories that were infused with his great sense of humor, and stayed in touch with friends. "He was a kind of genius," Engelhart said.

He was diagnosed with throat cancer in the middle of last year. He had treatments, and his friends were hopeful, but by early this year the cancer had spread to his lungs.

In the past two weeks, Riegel's friends and bandmates were able to visit him in Madison and say their good-byes. There were quite a few there Sunday, the day before he died, and in that moment Mike Riegel managed a remarkable rally. For a few hours he was Dr. Bop again, telling jokes and stories, enjoying his friends.

"It was his last show," Bob Kenison said.

Tuesday, March 1, 2005

Parks Was Often Angry, Often Right

It couldn't have been 10 days ago that I asked someone in the newsroom, "What's up with Gene Parks?"

It had struck me that I hadn't heard from Gene in months, and that was unusual. My newsroom friend hadn't heard anything lately, either. We sort of shrugged and moved on.

I wish I had pursued it. I might have had a last chance to talk to Gene, who died on Monday at 57.

We weren't close friends, but we had known each other a long time. Twenty-five years ago I spent a lot of time with Gene when I wrote a cover story on him for the Madison newspaper *City Lights*, an early 1980s competitor of *Isthmus*. The editor, David Chandler, titled it "The Devil and Eugene Parks." That seemed harsh, but Gene by then was controversial.

He lived his life in the public eye, and at first the

spotlight seemed like a good fit. The earliest headlines came in 1963, when Gene was a junior at La Follette. He and his twin sister were the first blacks to attend that high school. He wrote an impassioned letter to the editor of the *State Journal* on the subject of racism and civil rights, saying he might leave the country if the situation didn't improve. He received an outpouring of support, and his picture was in the paper. A short time later, he was elected president of the Wisconsin Association of Student Councils.

The future seemed to be all his. Gene brought passion and intelligence and political skills—he was a champion debater in high school and college—to the public arena in a city seemingly predisposed to receive him favorably. He won election to the City Council while still a college student.

Over the next decade, though, Gene Parks and Madison were increasingly at odds. He was one of the first— though hardly the last—to suggest that Madison's liberal reputation was more talk than action. In the 1970s he attacked establishment liberals like Mayor Paul Soglin and Police Chief David Couper for being slow on minority hiring. He did not always manage his personal life as well as he might have, and his celebrity made him an easy target for those who did not like him.

I remember when I did that *City Lights* story profile of Gene in the early 1980s, I had phoned his wife to get her perspective. She politely declined to participate in the story. "I don't think this is the right time for a big story on Eugene," she said.

But Gene either would not or could not leave the public eye. He may have lost elections, but he never lost his voice. He worked for Monroe Swan in the state capitol, and then in 1979, Ed Durkin, the Madison fire chief and a man willing to play a hunch, hired Gene in a top administrative post in the fire department.

In 1985, a new Madison mayor, Joe Sensenbrenner, hired Parks as the city's affirmative action officer. By April

1988 Parks had created so many waves in the job—accusing UW–Madison and city officials of being slow to recognize racism on a number of fronts—that the *State Journal* ran a story wondering if Parks would be fired.

Recalling that frenzied time, I once wrote, "I don't know who Sensenbrenner thought he was getting, but he got a passionate and flawed man who spoke loud and often on the subject of race."

Later that year, in October 1988, Gene and I were having a drink in the old Fess bar when someone from the city attorney's office entered and handed Gene a letter from Sensenbrenner telling Parks he was fired. Gene was outraged both by his dismissal and how it was handled. He immediately resolved to get even and filed a lawsuit. I wrote later:

"The bitter feud with Sensenbrenner and city officialdom eventually earned Parks a settlement of close to half a million dollars, but the personal cost of the battle was huge. I remember visiting him in the mid-1990s in his dad's old bar, Mr. P's, which by then was closed. Gene blew some dust off a whiskey bottle and we sat and talked surrounded by enormous stacks of court briefs and transcripts. It looked like a command bunker and Parks spoke as if besieged. He was angry. By then, that was his natural condition."

That was true, I think, but Gene also had a wonderful sense of humor and one of the loudest laughs I have ever heard. I remember a few years ago on a slow day I had invited readers to suggest how many Madisonians it would take to change a light bulb. I got dozens of responses, but only one actual person was named. "Just one," somebody wrote. "Gene Parks can talk a light bulb into its socket."

Gene called and said, "After all these years, I'm a light bulb joke?" But then he let out that great laugh.

When Gene resigned from his last city job—a position in the sign shop of Traffic Engineering, after a judge ruled Sensenbrenner had fired him illegally—he called me exactly two minutes after submitting his resignation. It was an early morning in June 2002. "There is no controversy. I was not asked to resign. I just decided that after nearly 24 years, it is time for me to move on." He paused, and in true Gene Parks fashion, said, "I intend to announce my candidacy for mayor next week."

Now we are left to ponder his legacy. It's mixed, but considerable. When he was comforting the afflicted, Gene was great. When he sought to afflict the comfortable— sometimes passing on unsubstantiated rumors—he was less than great.

I remember Nelson Algren, the fiercely talented Chicago writer, saying that to knock a city, you first have to earn the right by proving you care about it.

Over four decades, nobody in Madison earned that right more than Gene Parks.

━━━━━

Friday, March 11, 2005

The Gobbler Was One of a Kind

Last weekend I was with a small group of people at Babe's watching the Badgers wipe the floor with Purdue.

Because the game wasn't close, our conversation drifted, and someone was bemoaning having to drive to Milwaukee later that day.

"And you can't even stop at the Gobbler," I said.

"At the what?" She was young —in her 20s.

"You mean you haven't heard of the Gobbler?"

"What's the Gobbler?"

The short—and spectacularly incomplete—answer is

that the Gobbler was a motel and restaurant strategically located about halfway between Milwaukee and Madison, in Johnson Creek, just off Interstate 94.

But the Gobbler, which opened in 1967, was more than that. With its pink shag carpeting, vinyl chairs, and interior waterfall, it was a legend of kitsch. The favorite part of it for me was the rotating bar, which was just what it sounds like: The bar in the restaurant revolved electronically. You didn't really notice it as you sat there, but a friend of mine once went to the men's room and panicked when he came out. Having forgotten that the bar moved, he thought his group had left without him.

But the revolving bar was just a tiny bit of the Gobbler's unique lure.

This is how Minneapolis writer James Lileks introduced the Gobbler on a "tribute" website:

"What were they thinking?

"Imagine the pitch to investors:

"'It's going to be a futuristic, state-of-the-art motel with every modern convenience from water beds to 8-tracks. The entire dining area will be covered in deep-pile pink and purple carpet. But wait—here's the best part. It will look like an abstract sculpture of a giant turkey. We'll bill it as a romantic getaway—and call it the Gobbler!'"

A couple of years later, Lileks updated the site and noted: "Since I posted this site . . . I've heard from Gobbler fans all around the country. In a way, I'm deeply gratified to learn that the Gobbler lives in people's memories, and that other folks have discovered its jaw-dropping banality through this site."

That was 1999. There is now a more complete and at least somewhat more sincere tribute site, which you can access at www.gobblermotel.blogspot.com.

The site was put together by a woman named Lenka Reznicek, who, I was pleased to learn, is a staff assistant in the economics department at the University of Chicago.

Surrounded by Reality

Gobbler aficionados cut across all class and cultural lines.

"I had heard about it before I moved to the Chicago area," Reznicek told me when I reached her Thursday. "A friend of mine who appreciates anything offbeat told me about it. Then when I moved here I realized it was just a couple of hours away."

Reznicek drove up with friends in October 2001. Neither the restaurant nor the motel was operational by then, but she was able to take dozens of interior and exterior photos that are up on her site (and supplemented by promotional material from the Gobbler's heyday).

The timing of Reznicek's visit was important because when she came back again, in February 2002, she found to her dismay that the motel was gone, replaced by a bit of rubble and a hole in the ground. "The fire department torched it for a practice burn," Reznicek said. "I was glad I had taken those photos."

The restaurant reopened briefly in 2002 under a new name—the Round Stone Restaurant and Lounge—but it wasn't the same, and it didn't last.

One living link to the Gobbler is its original architect, Helmut Ajango, who is still in business in Fort Atkinson. He said the restaurant's name came because of the owner's vocation.

"Clarence Hartwig approached us in 1965 or '66," Ajango told me Thursday. "He was raising turkeys and evidently doing real well. He wanted to get out of the turkey business and into the restaurant business. He liked what we had done with the Fireside, which is a dinner theater today. He said he wanted a better design than the Fireside."

Ajango said the restaurant was completed in 1967, and the motel a few years after that. Actually, he said, the motel was never really completed—he had designed it to be circular, and it wound up semicircular. The restaurant, with its grand canopied carport entrance, was finished.

"I loved the revolving bar," I told him.

"There was only one other one in the country, in Seattle, when we did it," Ajango said. "At first, it went all the way around in 40 minutes, and some people got disoriented. We settled on an hour and 20 minutes."

Ajango said, "That writer, Lileks, said the restaurant was designed to look like a turkey. It was not. If he looks at it and sees a turkey, he has quite an imagination."

The most recent owners exhibited quite an imagination as well, when in September 2003 they went to the Johnson Creek Plan Commission with the idea of turning the restaurant into "The Gobbler A-Go-Go." According to a newspaper account at the time, the plan "would have the restaurant and bar feature go-go dancers wearing bikinis and dancing in cages, plus waitresses in Playboy bunny outfits."

The Plan Commission voted it down 7-0.

For now, the Gobbler lives only on the Internet and in memory, ever pink, plush—and revolving.

≡≡≡

Monday, March 28, 2005

Sheboygan Rascal Is at It Again

I was pleased to see Edmond Hou-Seye back in the news this month, even if the shenanigans that got him there were a mere shadow of his more inspired efforts of days gone by.

On March 7, Hou-Seye, 78, of Sheboygan, was found guilty of illegally reproducing a state disabled parking identification card.

Presumably Hou-Seye's brain was not doing its best work when he took 48 copies of the disabled parking card into a print shop in downtown Sheboygan and placed an order to have them laminated.

Doesn't everybody try to get four dozen disabled parking passes laminated at once? Apparently not. A print shop clerk alerted the manager, who alerted police.

Hou-Seye was fined $200 and court costs, and announced immediately he would appeal. "I have no intention of paying one cent of tribute to those scoundrels," he said.

Faking disabled parking cards is pretty low, and probably would have been beneath Hou-Seye in his heyday—although maybe not.

A Sheboygan native, Hou-Seye first burst onto the public stage in 1970 when he served as the "guru" for a Democratic candidate for secretary of state. Hou-Seye was a guru, all right. He wouldn't let his candidate, Robert A. Zimmermann, speak at all.

It is important to insert another piece of information here. The incumbent secretary of state at the time was a popular Republican named Robert C. Zimmerman.

Robert A. Zimmermann pumped gas at one of several of the stations Hou-Seye owned in the Sheboygan area. Hou-Seye rather quietly managed to get his employee on the ballot in the Democratic primary for secretary of state. His opponent was an up-and-coming Democrat named Tom Fox, who would one day become commissioner of insurance in Wisconsin.

Zimmermann, the gas station employee, defeated Fox in the September 8, 1970, primary, an outcome that a young *Capital Times* reporter—Dave Zweifel by name—called "one of the most amazing election stories of the century."

There was no question voters had mistaken the name on the Democratic primary ballot for the incumbent Republican, which does not speak highly of the electorate. Still, the result stood: Zimmermann would face Zimmerman in November.

Reporters trying to reach the upstart Zimmermann

were directed to his guru, Edmond Hou-Seye. "I speak for Bob," Hou-Seye said. "Bob can't be reached. He's a bachelor, you know, and he has a country retreat where he can't be reached."

Two weeks after the primary, two newspaper reporters who were also good friends, Frank Ryan of UPI and Jim Selk of the *Wisconsin State Journal,* drove from Madison to Sheboygan to try to get a word with the candidate, Zimmermann.

They found him collecting money from customers at a self-service gas station in Cedar Grove. "You must speak to Mr. Hou-Seye," he said.

But how can you run for office and not speak? the reporters asked.

"Richard Nixon had his strategy and I have mine," Zimmermann said.

Selk and Ryan found Hou-Seye knocking back one old-fashioned after another at a Sheboygan saloon called the Big Apple. The reporters introduced themselves.

"Journalism is the science of distortion," Hou-Seye said.

While the reporters mulled that over, Hou-Seye said, "I can drink anyone in Sheboygan under the table."

Selk later offered this description of Hou-Seye: "A likable, articulate, highly intelligent egotist with a remarkable capacity for old-fashioneds."

When Zimmermann lost to the real Zimmerman in the general election, Selk got in touch with the guru to ask what he would do next. "I'm looking for a man named William Proxmire," Hou-Seye said.

That didn't pan out, and instead Hou-Seye began running for office himself. His most publicized effort was probably his unsuccessful race against incumbent Tony Earl in the 1986 Democratic primary for governor.

It was about that time that Hou-Seye began using a billboard on his property to weigh in on various issues and public officials, a tactic that resulted in a defamation charge after Mayor Jelly Belly appeared on the board.

In 1996, contractors hired by the DNR "raided" one of Hou-Seye's properties, Poor Edmond's Tire Shop, to remove the 60,000 old tires that had accumulated there. The tires were a fire hazard and breeding ground for mosquitoes and worse, but by then Hou-Seye had other worries associated with the shop.

It turned out Hou-Seye owed $177,000 in back taxes on the property. His excuse? Poor Edmond's Tire Shop was really the Research Universal Life Church, and thus exempt from taxes.

Through it all, Hou-Seye seemingly never lost his faith in the electoral process. Just last month he took out nomination papers to enter the primary for mayor of Sheboygan. He didn't make the ballot, however, when it developed he hadn't filed the 200 necessary signatures.

It's not like he didn't have a couple of hundred people who would have signed. Asked this month why he wanted 48 disabled parking ID cards, Hou-Seye explained they were for family members to use when they drove him around town.

━━━━━━━━━
━━━━━━━━━

Tuesday, March 29, 2005

Idea Came to Him on Visions

I think I may have a solution for the vexing problem of the new strip joint in Pine Bluff.

Most people are aware that Hot Rods, which opened recently in the unincorporated town, has been highly controversial, in part because it is located two blocks from St. Mary's of Pine Bluff Catholic Church.

On Friday, however, my colleague Samara Kalk Derby broke the news that the pastor of the church, Rick Heilman, has been leading his congregation in praying for a miracle—that the strip club will go away.

"We know that it's going to take a miracle to get them out of here but we are hopeful that God will provide that," Heilman said.

About 10 days ago, some 300 people gathered at the church and set up a mile-long row of 14 crosses—the Stations of the Cross—one of which is directly across from Hot Rods.

It's clear that the pastor and his congregation are genuinely upset about the presence of the strip club in Pine Bluff.

Some people just don't like strip clubs. Many years ago, Roger Simon, then a columnist for the *Chicago Sun-Times*, noted in an introduction to his collected columns that when he went away to college, his mother told him she didn't care what he did with his life, as long as he didn't play the trumpet in a strip joint.

On graduating, Simon told his mother he was going to be a newspaperman.

She sent him a trumpet.

Some people just don't like newspaper reporters, either.

My idea for Pine Bluff is inspired by something that happened five years ago involving a Madison church and the unusual venue it had chosen for its services.

It all started in September 1999 when a Madison engineer who worked for a large local firm was distributing leaflets on Madison's east side for the "Celebration '99" Christian gala that was to be held the following month at the Dane County Coliseum. The engineer and his wife had been members of a conservative congregation in Madison, but recently they had joined Common Ground, a nondenominational church that rented space from the East Madison Community Center.

The engineer explained all this to me later, when we had lunch at the Avenue Bar.

While spreading the word about the Coliseum celebration, the engineer had dropped a leaflet at a residence near Visions, the venerable Madison strip joint on East Washington Avenue.

It was while walking from that home, the engineer said, that an idea came into his head. "I felt the Lord had laid upon me a command," he said.

What was the command?

"That I should find the owner of Visions and tell him that God loves him."

The engineer said that when he first heard the command, he tried to ignore it. But God's voice was persistent and over the next few days he kept hearing the command: "Find the owner of Visions and tell him that God loves him."

After a week or so of this, the engineer ran it by his wife. "She was supportive, which surprised me," he said. He reasoned it had something to do with the fact that their church made a point of reaching out to those whom the engineer described as "broken people with broken lives. Ex-offenders, substance abusers. . . . The church is about God loving you, no matter who or what you are."

Some church members were skeptical. Why, they asked, do you want to talk to the owner of Visions?

"We know God loves him, whoever he is."

The engineer began leaving notes and phone messages for the owner of Visions. After a couple of days the owner, Tom Reichenberger, phoned the engineer. "Who are you? And what do you want?"

The engineer said, "I think God wants me to meet with you and tell you something. Might we have lunch?"

Reichenberger was reluctant and asked for more details.

The engineer replied, "I believe the Lord has asked me to tell you he loves you."

It was at this moment that the engineer dropped the other shoe. "And to ask if you'd be willing to open your building up to hosting worship services."

Reichenberger said, "Well, I've been in business 25 years and no one has ever asked me that."

The two set up a lunch at Pedro's and ironed out the details.

And every other Sunday for 18 months, church services were held Sunday afternoons at Visions. Quilts were hung over some of Visions' wall art. One Sunday the place was absolutely jammed and a local Christian singing group performed along with a nine-car caravan from the Richland Center Fellowship that included actors and dancers.

"I looked around," the engineer told me, "and everyone was dancing to the praise and glory of the Lord. I had tears streaming down my face."

It's something for Pine Bluff—the people on both sides of the controversy—to think about.

Some time later, I asked Reichenberger why the Visions services had stopped, and he wasn't certain, though the engineer had once told me, "Every time we have to ask ourselves: Is that what we should be doing?"

For quite a while, it was. "I think God wants us to use that place and that ministry to bring people there who would normally never go near a church setting," the engineer said. "It's about letting people know they are loved. My wife and I used to drive by and pray that it would be destroyed. Now I pray that it will be used by God as a powerful ministry."

━━━━━━━━━━
━━━━━━━━━━
━━━━━━━━━━

Monday, April 4, 2005

Schiro Golf Tales a Link to Past

Open George Schiro's golf bag and eight decades of memories come tumbling out with the Titleists.

He can tell you about the time Walter Hagen played Monona, or Arnold Palmer killed a drive on what is now No. 16 at Odana, or about the time, in the 1940s, when he, Schiro, made the mistake of trying to take Ben Hogan's picture on the driving range of the Tam O'Shanter Country Club in Chicago.

He can tell you about any of that, but in a life in golf maybe there has never been a better time than when he was just a kid, caddying at Nakoma, and the caddies could play for free on Mondays.

"We'd get up before it was light and have 72 holes in before noon," Schiro was saying Sunday. "We'd play barefoot, with three or four clubs, just hit it and run. We had to be off the golf course by noon."

There is something of that barefoot kid still in George Schiro, who turns 80 on Tuesday. You sense it when you see him helping young golfers, as I've seen him with my son. Somehow he speaks their language. Maybe it's just that the kids can spot the mischief in Schiro's 80-year-old eyes. Listen to what I'm telling you, those eyes say, or you might find yourself in a match playing barefoot with four clubs with your allowance on the line, and you know who is walking away with the cash? Not you.

Schiro may be best remembered around here for the decade or so he spent running the city-owned golf shops at both Yahara Hills and Odana Hills in the 1970s. His parting with the city was not amicable—I give the city a double bogey in the deal, though I'm biased—but Schiro landed on his feet teaching and talking golf, as he always has.

Now George's wife, Pat, is putting together a party in celebration of George's 80th. The details have just been finalized and the party is April 17, from 3 to 6 p.m. at the Nakoma Golf Club.

"The world is invited," Pat says.

It should be a delightful event, and good tonic for George, who is still getting over the loss of his great friend Steve Caravello, who died last year. Caravello was the best amateur golfer in Madison history, but more than that, he and Schiro are links to a fading era—a time of blade irons, steak houses, and Sinatra albums, when male friendship meant golf but also gruff humor, side bets, whiskey afterward, and stories, always stories.

Nobody seems to have time for that anymore, and what business do I have getting sentimental about it? Times change. Hell, today even Schiro has a cell phone.

He couldn't have imagined that 80 years ago, not in that old house in the 800 block of Regent Street, where he was born in 1925. George's dad worked for Madison Gas and Electric then, and he worked hard, digging ditches for their power lines.

When Prohibition was repealed in the early 1930s, his dad opened Schiro's Tavern on Regent, one block from the house, and that lasted a long time, decades, until the brilliant urban planners decided to get rid of Madison's Greenbush neighborhood.

George was long out of the house by then. His life's passion arrived by accident one day when he was walking with some kids to go swimming in the lake. George figures he was 12, maybe 13. An adult of his acquaintance, local businessman Jerry Onheiber, was hitting golf balls in a field near the beach. Would George like to shag them for him, for

25 cents?

Schiro did. Before long he was caddying for Onheiber at the now-departed Burr Oaks Golf Course off South Park Street. From there he looped at Blackhawk and Nakoma, until finally—after a stint in the Navy—Nakoma pro George Vitense offered Schiro a job as his assistant.

Since then, you'd be hard pressed to find a job in golf that George Schiro hasn't held. He's taught, made and fit clubs, run courses and ranges. There was the day in the 1970s when he was in the shop at Yahara and an old man came in and asked for a cool drink. They got to chatting and the man asked, "Are you a PGA pro?" Schiro said that he was. "Me, too," the man said.

He was a pro, all right. The man was Johnny Farrell, who had an adult child living in McFarland at the time. Farrell had come to visit and found his way to nearby Yahara, where he found Schiro, a student of the game who knew that in 1928 Johnny Farrell had shocked the golf world by beating Bobby Jones in a 36-hole playoff for the United States Open at Olympia Fields in Chicago. Farrell was from the era of stories, too. "He talked about Jones, Hagen, Gene Sarazen," Schiro recalled. "He must have been 80 years old by then."

It was at another course in Chicago, on the range of Tam O'Shanter in Chicago—where Byron Nelson won one of his remarkable 11 straight tournaments in 1945—that Schiro spotted the legendary Ben Hogan hitting balls on the range next to fellow pro Lloyd Mangrum. Schiro was excited. Nobody swung the club like Hogan. If Schiro wanted a life in golf, he should get a picture of Hogan's swing. He pulled out his camera but Hogan growled, "Get out of here."

Mangrum laughed. "You can take my picture."

"Cut it out, Lloyd," Hogan said.

Schiro grinned and moved on. He missed the picture, but he got the life.

Monday, May 30, 2005

Sunsets and Great Memories

The Memorial Union has announced plans for a "sunset celebration" on the terrace this summer, Saturday nights starting June 11.

The celebration is patterned after the nightly sunset ritual in Key West, Florida, where tourists and assorted oddballs gather on the Mallory Square waterfront to toast the day's end and gaze at the color-splashed dusk sky.

The Union's affable marketing guy, Marc Kennedy, called to ask if I'd be interested in being one of a series of "celebrity" sunset toasters. Mayor Dave Cieslewicz will handle the first duty June 11.

I told Marc that these days the summer sunset is close to my bedtime. But his call and mention of Key West took me back more than 25 years to the summer of 1979 and one of the best things I ever did for myself. I relate it here in part because if any young people happen to be reading this and are on the fence about whether or not to embark on an adventure—well, read on.

I had just graduated from UW–Madison—it took five years and two summer sessions, but I made it, barely, with a B.A. in English—and was determined to try to earn a living as a writer.

At the time I had written two professional articles— that is, I had been paid for them. I had done a freelance piece on Badger hockey for *Madison* magazine ($50) and a book review for the *Milwaukee Journal* ($30).

Looking back, those appear to be scant credentials. But

213

Surrounded by Reality

I remember like yesterday the letter from the *Journal*'s book editor, Bob Wells, saying he would like to publish the review I had submitted of Thomas McGuane's novel *Panama*.

"We don't usually accept over-the-transom reviews," Wells wrote. "But I am making an exception this time."

My first sale. I have had a lot of ups and downs as a writer since then, but I don't know if I've ever been more excited than I was that night.

During my last weeks at UW–Madison, I had formed the vague idea that upon graduating, I wanted to take a trip someplace before coming back to Madison and beginning my "career," such as it was.

I had a little money in the bank and a burning desire to see one place in particular—Key West.

The reasons were linked to the career. I loved the sun and the ocean, but Key West was also a literary town—Ernest Hemingway had called it home for most of the 1930s. Tom McGuane—the writer I most admired in college—had followed Hemingway there, and McGuane's 1972 novel, *Ninety-Two in the Shade,* set in Key West, had knocked me out.

It was McGuane's sheer writing skill—his sentences exploded off the page. Consider this passage from *Ninety-Two*, about the electrocution of Charlie Starkweather: "Restaurants darkened and Starkweather went off like a flashbulb at Tricia's wedding. It reduced his bulk through vaporization. He no longer fitted the electrical collar. They found him in the goodbye room like a wind-torn 1890 umbrella. A year later he might have grown Virginia creeper like a grape stake. After each electrocution, the officials of the republic get together for a real down-home Christian burial out of that indomitable American conviction that even God likes fried food."

It didn't hurt that Key West also meant Jimmy Buffett (McGuane's brother-in-law), whose best song, "A Pirate Looks at Forty," was an ode to a (real) Key West drug smuggler coming to the end of the line. As McGuane has noted, Key West was always a favorite of pirates.

214

The Best of Doug Moe on Madison

I flew down that June and stayed all summer. I rented a room in a house on Whalton Street owned by a Brazilian divorcee named Tulita Beal. There was a mango tree in the front yard. It was a 10-minute walk to Captain Tony's and Sloppy Joe's, Hemingway's bars, and only a minute from the Casa Marina, a classic hotel being refurbished by Marriott. I found a $100 bill on the floor of the bar there.

I also met a young woman who had been sent to Key West from Boston by Marriott to help with the launch of the renovated Casa Marina. She lived in a suite and had signing privileges at all the bars and restaurants in the hotel. A good person to know. She was an aspiring photographer, too, and took pictures for the stories I worked on that summer. She got a photographer credit for a picture of the Hemingway house for a story I sold freelance to the *Capital Times*.

We went more than once together to see the sunset. It was a magical summer, and one night when the sun almost seemed to break against the horizon, seeping color into the low wispy clouds, we talked about staying. In the end, we didn't. She went home to Boston and I came home to Madison.

It was on my connecting flight home, in Chicago, that I wound up sitting next to a nice woman who, on finding out my desire to be a writer, told me she was on the board of directors of *Wisconsin Trails* magazine. She said she was starting a magazine of her own, for girls, and asked if I would write a story explaining football to girls for $50.

I did, though I told her I thought she was wrong to be excluding half of her potential readers. Why stick just to girls?

Some years later, my airplane seatmate, Pleasant Rowland, sold her company, devoted to girls, for $700 million. I never heard from her again. I never heard from my Boston friend again, either. But I think I might go down to the Union Terrace one Saturday night this summer, and remember.

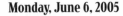

Boom Box Parade Is Ours First

A passing mention by a friend of a "boom box orchestra" at New York's River to River Festival over the weekend has led me to the shocking discovery that a small city in Connecticut is taking credit for a Madison invention.

At least I think it is a Madison invention. We'll take credit unless someone proves otherwise, and we can certainly claim we deserve it over Willimantic, Connecticut.

The mention of the boom boxes on parade at the New York festival will bring back memories for many Madisonians. I was nostalgic enough to go on the internet Sunday, and that's where I unearthed the disturbing claim being perpetrated by Willimantic.

I found this story posted on a blog July 12, 2004: "The Boombox Parade has its origins in parody. In 1986, the city of Willimantic did not have the money to put a marching band into its Independence Day Parade. Formerly the thread-making capital of the United States, Willimantic is a city that has seen hard times for decades. A local woman, Kathy Clark, got the idea of having spectators bring their boom boxes, all tuned to the same radio station, playing patriotic music at full blast while a random assortment of people and groups march down the street."

That radio station, WILI/AM, has a similar story on its website, although it says that it was actually the 1986 Memorial Day parade, and that it went off without music, which led to a change for the Independence Day parade: "Five weeks later, the Boom Box Parade concept was born, as WILI plays the marching band music on the air, while thousands march and watch, loudly playing their radios (boom boxes)."

The phrase to note there is: "Five weeks later, the Boom Box Parade concept was born."

I think not.

Madison residents with a bit of institutional memory will remember the name Leon Varjian. At last report a few years ago, Varjian was a middle-aged math teacher in New Jersey. But in the late 1970s and into the '80s, Varjian was an inspired Madison prankster. With co-conspirator Jim Mallon, Varjian ran for Wisconsin student government office on the Pail and Shovel party ticket. Among their campaign promises was to move the Statue of Liberty to Madison.

Naturally, they won. And they brought the statue to Madison. Or at least a replica of the top of the statue, made of chicken wire, muslin, and paint. They put it on the ice on Lake Mendota and claimed the helicopter cable carrying the statue had broken and the statue had crashed through the ice with only the top exposed.

Another of Varjian's well-known pranks involved putting more than 1,000 pink flamingoes on Bascom Hill, under the cover of darkness.

But it was April Fools' Day—April 1, 1982—that prompted one of Varjian's most inspired stunts, and also a memorable photo caption that ran under the picture taken by *Cap Times* photographer Hank Koshollek. The caption:

"Thousands of amateur April fools were left gasping with envy Thursday as professional yuk Leon Varjian upstaged them all—proving himself once again the undisputed major domo of the bizarre. Varjian is the former Wisconsin Student Association vice president responsible for bringing the Statue of Liberty to Lake Mendota and bombing other Big Ten campuses with sacks of cow dung. Though now a mild-mannered state bureaucrat, Varjian can never resist the yearly lure of All Fools Day.

Surrounded by Reality

"With the order, 'Musicians, shoulder your boom boxes,' he led a 22-piece radio-toting band on a march down State Street. The band, decked out in discarded Indiana University uniforms Varjian once bought at an auction, marched to the music of John Phillip Sousa, compliments of WORT radio. The ragtag regiment halted at a small park in the 600 block of State Street, where Varjian gave thanks that a freak snowstorm had been cleared just in time for the spectacle."

You will note the Madison parade happened more than four years before the "Boom Box Parade concept was born," according to WILI.

It is true that Willimantic has carried on its boom box parade tradition longer than Madison did.

There was a second parade in Madison, in June 1983, again led by Varjian. Mayor Joe Sensenbrenner participated—dressed in a tux—and three local radio stations carried the music. American of Madison and Rayovac contributed boom boxes and batteries, and the city's Committee for the Arts put up $500 to cover additional costs.

The next year, however, the boom went bust in Madison. A 1984 *Capital Times* story reported: "This year, the city's cupboard is bare. Unless a sponsor is found, there will be no Boom Box Parade."

Ed Janus, then general manager of the local minor league baseball team and a free spirit himself, said, "Poor Leon is a prophet—and a prophet in his own city is never appreciated. I think Leon should take the Boom Box to Chicago."

Two years later, Willimantic had its first boom box parade, and they're still having them every July 4, with regular coverage from national news organizations.

Varjian went not to Chicago but to New Jersey.

Before he left, however, Varjian wrote a column for the *Capital Times* with this lead: "There's a curse on my house! My city is invaded! Everything I have done is being undone!"

And what had Leon so upset? The fact Madison was hosting the national drum and bugle corps championships—live musicians with real instruments, the antithesis of Varjian's mechanized boom box dream.

"They're spoiling everything," he wrote.

Thursday, June 30, 2005

"Fit Man" Lets Good Times Roll

This is a good time to be Bobby Hinds, the irrepressible portable gym exercise guru who could give Donald Trump lessons in self-promotion.

On Tuesday evening, Hinds took delivery of a vintage Rolls-Royce automobile that was first purchased by the late comedian Jack Benny in 1958 as a Christmas present for his wife.

Wednesday morning, Hinds was posing by the blue and silver classic car in his newest incarnation, "The Fit Man," a faux gangster who is actually a reincarnation of an earlier Hinds persona.

Hinds first came up with his violin case-toting character a decade ago. Since then Hinds has had an extended correspondence with the late John Gotti, a real gangster, lending Bobby's impersonation a certain cachet. Besides, it's fun. Well into his 70s, Bobby Hinds wants to get out again among the people and do what he has always done best, which is to sell his portable gym and whatever else needs selling. Mostly, Bobby is selling himself.

He's doing it better than ever today, as you might guess from the Rolls and the downtown penthouse condominium he purchased recently while keeping his longtime home on the near west side.

Bobby's Lifeline gyms have been selling like popsicles at the equator. One cable TV infomercial alone moved 410,000 gyms during a single month last summer. Now Bobby is looking forward to commissioning a biography of himself. The only question is whether one volume will be enough to handle the job.

The Rolls is a good example. It was a month or so ago that Hinds was thumbing through an issue of *Hemmings Motor News* and noticed a Rolls-Royce for sale that had at one time belonged to Muhammad Ali. Hinds, a former boxing champion, was intrigued. But as he kept reading he found another car with an equally impressive pedigree, and before long Hinds was in touch with the dealer in State College, Pennsylvania, who was advertising the car.

Jack Galloway, general manager of the dealership, said Wednesday that they acquired the Rolls about six years ago from a Pennsylvania couple who had bought it out of Hollywood.

Galloway got in touch with Rolls-Royce and learned that the car's history included the fact that Jack Benny had bought it in late 1958. The cost: $38,706.

"They keep impeccable records," Galloway said.

Hinds, asked what he paid for the car this week, replied, "Six figures."

Whatever he paid, Hinds figures the car will earn the money back in public relations, and he's probably right. It has a buzz factor, and Hinds was an expert on creating buzz before anyone knew the word.

In the 1970s, Hinds was demonstrating his Lifeline gym—the gyms use rubber tubing to create resistance and, unlike weights, fit easily in a violin case—for a couple dozen laid-over passengers in Chicago's O'Hare Airport when CBS newsman Charles Kuralt ambled by. The result of that chance meeting was one of the longest *On the Road* segments—12-1/2 minutes—Kuralt ever aired.

Similarly, Hinds was having a drink in Sardi's, the famous New York theater bar, when someone made the mistake of asking what Bobby did for a living, and out came the portable Lifeline Gym. "Mistake" isn't the right word. It's just that if you were in Sardi's that night and thought a Broadway play was the only performance you would see, you couldn't have been more wrong. Of course Hinds demonstrated his gym. Would you ask a bird not to fly or a fish not to swim? People set down their martini glasses and watched.

After Bobby was done, a guy in a nice-looking suit came over and said, "You could use that in a small place, couldn't you?"

"Sure," Hinds said.

The man handed Hinds a $50 bill and a name and address in Illinois. The name was John Gotti, and the address was the federal prison in Marion.

Bobby sent the gym—this was 1998—and a few weeks later it came back with a letter, handwritten in neat script, from Gotti, the "Dapper Don" of New York City who was famous for being well-dressed when he ordered people killed.

Gotti wrote: "We aren't allowed any exercise equipment at this prison—in fact, we aren't allowed much of anything! This is a lock-down prison, and so we don't even have a chair in our cells—the beds are poured concrete platforms—so I'm sure you can imagine why your Lifeline Gym is a no-no. But it was very thoughtful and classy of you to send one—thank you! As for my exercise routine, I do lots of push-ups, step-ups, and running in place, which is easy as we are in our cells 22 hours every day. I feel great. Again, I hope this finds you well and with good mind-set. Sincerely, John Gotti."

Hinds and Gotti continued to correspond until the gangster's death a few years ago. Now there is a new "gangster" loose in the land, and he's driving a Rolls-Royce. "I feel like this is my second wind," said Bobby Hinds, the only Bobby Hinds there has ever been or ever will be. "I'm in better shape than I was 30 years ago."

Inevitably, Hinds was asked what's up for him next.

"I'm going on MTV," he said.

═══════

Thursday, July 7, 2005

Critics Aside, Wisconsin Is Burger Heaven

There is a vast left-wing conspiracy loose in the land against what constitutes a good cheeseburger.

I am pleased to be able to expose it and heap upon it the ridicule it deserves. I'd rather heap ketchup and onions, but ridicule will do.

The conspiracy consists of an article by Alan Richman, "The 20 Hamburgers You Must Eat Before You Die," in the July issue of *GQ* magazine, and a review by Virginia Heffernan this week in the *New York Times* of a George Motz documentary film, "Hamburger America," which debuted Monday night on the Sundance Channel.

I will address the *GQ* piece first. It is a blasphemy. It would have been bad enough if Richman, whom I peg as an East Coast elitist snob, just ignored Madison and Wisconsin. The state is home to the Hamburger Hall of Fame in Seymour, where the hamburger was invented in 1885. Madison is home to the Hamburger King, Jeff Stanley of Dotty's, as well as other memorable burgers—the Plaza burger, the Gritty burger—that enjoy a national reputation.

But not only did Richman ignore Madison, he lashed out at the entire state of Wisconsin, and one famed Milwaukee area burger joint in particular.

In his story, Richman noted that he traveled 23,750 miles and ate 162 burgers in 93 establishments. He included a sidebar to the main story titled "Worst Burger."

The "Worst Burger" sidebar begins: "Solly, may he rest in grease, is credited with inventing the butter burger, a much loved, much praised regional specialty. I walked into Solly's Grille near Milwaukee and asked for my burger with sautéed onion. I'm guessing, but I'd say it came with close to a half stick of butter soaked into the bun and the burger and finally pooled on the plate. It was like slurping dairy drainage. Wisconsin, the Dairy State, should be renamed the Death-by-Dairy State."

Heffernan, writing Monday in the *New York Times,* had this to say: "Solly's Grille in Glendale, Wis., smears its burgers with a thick layer of butter; they look unappetizing."

It's clear that these people live in fear of getting a grease stain on their designer clothes. Sending them out to judge cheeseburgers is like sending me to Paris to rate women's fashions.

For instance, one of Richman's immortal 20 burgers is something called the "California Burger" at Houston's in— where else?—Santa Monica.

"This burger had no flaws," Richman wrote. "Zero. The roll: soft and sweet, almost like brioche. . . . The condiment: a touch of honey-mustard dressing. Avocado and arugula are another great touch. Houston's California burger is a rainbow of colors."

Honey-mustard dressing? Brioche? Avocado? Arugula? I'd never heard of arugula. I now understand it is a salad green. Well, as P.J. O'Rourke once observed, lettuce is no good unless you can throw a head of it from home plate to second base.

Surrounded by Reality

Rainbow? Political correctness has indeed become totalitarian if it is infiltrating the culture of cheeseburgers.

A cheeseburger is supposed to be messy. If you can handle it with one napkin, it's automatically no good. Some years ago, writing about an anniversary of the Plaza Tavern, I received a bit of criticism from purists when I noted that the correct way to eat a Plaza cheeseburger is to order double Plaza sauce, and then smother that with ketchup and mustard.

It's a good sign if, when the waitress sets the burger in front of you, it slides off the plate. You will get a good view of this at the Plaza because, as Jeff Hagen, author of *Searching for the Holy Grill,* observed, you sink so far into those great old booths at the Plaza that when your burger arrives, it's at chin level.

The alternative to a great sauce is butter, the substance that so offended both Richman and Heffernan.

On the website roadfood.com, Paul E. Smith of Knoxville, Tennessee, notes: "It seems that a local specialty in Milwaukee is a butter burger. I had my first at Solly's. . . . It is impossible to hand eat one because the butter will run down your arm and grease up your elbow. After you OD on butter and burger and if there is room left, try their custard. You will have to have a wheelchair to get out."

Another visitor to the site said this: "I went to Solly's with my mom, when we went to Summerfest, the annual music festival. I had the double with cheese and a chocolate banana malt. After we ate it felt like I was going to fall into a coma."

A coma, a wheelchair—in the burger world, that's worth five stars.

Wednesday, July 27, 2005

A Different Triumph of the Will

The name of Howard Weiss lives in Wisconsin sports history. A Fort Atkinson native, born in 1917, Weiss enrolled at UW–Madison in 1935, and in 1938 was named the Big Ten's most valuable football player.

A punishing fullback who also played linebacker on defense, Weiss in 1938 finished sixth in the Heisman Trophy balloting.

"To this day," wrote Don Kopriva and Jim Mott in *On Wisconsin*, their history of UW athletics, "his 40-yard run against Northwestern in 1938 ranks as one of the greatest in Badger annals." Weiss was one of 35 Badger athletes named as charter members of the UW Athletic Hall of Fame in 1991. He died in Milwaukee in 1997, one month after his 80th birthday.

Weiss's name lives in Badger sports lore, and always will. Yet it also lives—literally lives—in the person of an 81-year-old man who 60 years ago uncovered the last will and testament of Adolf Hitler.

It is a long way from gridiron glory at Camp Randall to the bottom of a dry well in Germany and the final ravings of one of history's most reviled tyrants. But the connection was made Sunday in the *Washington Post Magazine* in an extraordinary 8,300-word article by Matthew Brzezinski.

As Brzezinski tells it, the tale begins in Germany with a boy named Hans Arnold Wangersheim, the son of a flamboyant sports columnist for a newspaper in Nuremburg.

In 1930 the boy was 6 and his world began to fall

225

apart. His parents' divorce was acrimonious. The father was for the most part gone with the wind, and the mother was unable to care for three children. "There was just not enough money to feed us," the boy told Brzezinski, decades later, for the *Post* story. "The girls needed to be protected, so I was the candidate to be placed in an orphanage."

He got along with other kids in the orphanage, but not with the Hitler Youth thugs who routinely roughed up Jewish orphans.

In 1938—the year of Howard Weiss's dazzling season at Camp Randall—the boy got lucky. He was chosen for a program, Kindertransport, that eventually "rescued thousands of Jewish children from the gas chamber," according to Brzezinski.

The boy arrived by boat in New York City: "He is 13 when he arrives in this country, with only a cardboard suitcase and $5 to his name. He does not speak a word of English or know a single soul."

The boy was put on a train to Chicago. "We got into Chicago at 3 a.m.," he told Brzezinski, "and I noticed a train departing for Milwaukee. I'd heard they spoke German there, so I got on and locked myself in the bathroom."

He was homeless for a time in Milwaukee, ended up in an orphanage from which he repeatedly decamped, and finally had the great good fortune to be matched with a loving foster family in Janesville. It was the start of a good period—"the happiest of my life," the boy would recall—and a new start demanded a new name. The boy settled on his middle name, Arnold, which he matched with the last name of the sporting hero in nearby Madison. What 13-year-old kid wouldn't idolize the Big Ten Conference player of the year? With that Hans Arnold Wangersheim became Arnold Weiss.

Howard Weiss, the football star, served two years in the Navy during World War II. By 1945, Arnold Weiss, the young immigrant, was himself in the service, a 21-year-old assigned to Germany with U.S. Army Counter Intelligence Corps (CIC).

By autumn 1945, Arnold Weiss's assignment had become more specific, and its unfolding is the most compelling part of Brzezinski's *Post* article. CIC had been asked to prove once and for all that Adolf Hitler was dead. Rumors to the contrary had grown rampant.

Weiss, based in Munich, recalled that a top Hitler aide, Martin Bormann, had as his adjutant a Munich man, Wilhelm Zander, still at large (as was Bormann). With the grudging help of Zander's mother, sister, and girlfriend, Weiss and a British colleague traced Zander to a farmhouse on the Czech border where he was living under an alias.

Weiss captured Zander, who had been in the now notorious final bunker with Hitler and Bormann, only leaving toward the end. "Why did you leave?" Weiss asked. "I was sent on an important mission as a courier," Zander said. "I suppose you want the documents." With that, Zander led Weiss to another farmhouse and a dry well in the back, from which he extracted his old SS uniform and a briefcase that contained a plain manila envelope, which Weiss ripped open.

It was Hitler's will, dated April 29, 1945, 4 a.m., and signed by Hitler, Bormann, and Joseph Goebbels. In the document, Hitler said he would take his own life rather than be "paraded around like a zoo exhibit," in Brzezinski's words.

It was as close as anyone had come to proving Hitler was truly dead, and Arnold Weiss won medals for its discovery. He moved on to hunt other Nazis, and eventually he went on to a highly successful career as an international investment executive in Washington, D.C., where he lives today.

Howard Weiss—who inspired the young German immigrant to take his name—succeeded after the war, too. He had played some pro football for the Detroit Lions but eventually went into insurance in Milwaukee. By age 39

Weiss was president of the Roberts Company, one of Wisconsin's largest insurers.

At the time of his death in 1997, Howard Weiss was recognized as one of Milwaukee's leading philanthropists, and why not? He had already made a present of his name.

———

Thursday, July 28, 2005

Interview with a Nazi Hunter

It turns out that Arnold Weiss, the Army Counter Intelligence Corps officer who found Adolf Hitler's will in a dry well in Germany late in 1945, has Madison connections beyond taking the name of Howard Weiss, a UW football star whom Weiss, as a teenager, had read about in the newspaper.

I related some of Weiss's story Wednesday, after reading a *Washington Post Magazine* cover story Sunday about his exploits chasing down Nazis in Europe after Hitler's fall.

It was of heightened interest here because when Weiss, 81, had come to this country as a child refugee from Germany in 1938, he landed in Janesville. At the suggestion of his foster brother there, the young immigrant changed his name from Hans Arnold Wangersheim to Arnold Hans Weiss. Howard Weiss was a star fullback with the Badgers, having won the Big Ten Conference most valuable player award in 1938.

I had been unable to reach Arnold Weiss earlier in the week, but Wednesday I did, at his office in Washington, D.C. Weiss was a founder of Emerging Markets Partnerships, "one of Washington's largest international investment firms," according to the *Post*, and though he celebrated his 81st birthday just a few days ago, he still goes into the office.

The *Post* described him like this: "Weiss is now officially—and grudgingly—retired, though you'd never know it, since he still gets up each morning, dons a tailored suit and drives his big Mercedes to EMP's offices on Pennsylvania Avenue. He's married and has two grown sons."

When I reached Weiss, he was pleased to talk about his years in Wisconsin, which he'd told the *Post* were "among the happiest of my life."

It turns out he is a UW–Madison graduate and continues a close relationship with the school. Most surprisingly, the foster family who welcomed Weiss in Janesville in the late 1930s turns out to have been named Wexler, and Weiss's foster brother was the late Jay Wexler, well-known in Madison as a jeweler, attorney, amateur actor, and outspoken member of the Madison City Council in the 1970s. Jay Wexler suffered a fatal heart attack here in 1980.

Weiss graduated from UW–Madison in 1951 with a degree in political science and followed that with a law degree in 1953. He has been an active alumnus, having once served on the Board of Visitors of the Law School.

Currently Weiss serves on the Board of Visitors of the UW department of astronomy, which together with Rutgers University and the South African Astronomical Observatory is building an enormously high-powered telescopic lens. Weiss says he offered to help "because I have an office in Johannesburg," and he wound up on the Board of Visitors.

It has been a life of remarkable achievement for a boy who arrived on American shores with $5 in his pocket and no knowledge of English. As I related Wednesday, Weiss escaped the Nazis in Germany with the help of Kindertransport. The boy took a train from New York to Chicago and then another train from Chicago to Milwaukee because he had heard people in Milwaukee speak German. "I was right," Weiss told me. "The police officer who picked me up there spoke German." From orphanages in Milwaukee he eventually wound up with the Wexlers in Janesville and, some years later, came to Madison for college.

Of course, it was those years before Weiss enrolled at UW–Madison, the years at the end of World War II in Europe, that led Washington writer Matthew Brzezinski to tell Weiss's extraordinary tale in Sunday's *Post Magazine.* Brzezinski's wife works for EMP, Weiss's company, and at a company picnic a few years ago the writer heard Weiss telling a bit of what it was like to be a CIC officer chasing fugitive Nazis after Germany's capitulation in 1945. The writer told Weiss if he ever wanted to talk about it for publication, he would be ready to listen. Recently, Weiss agreed to tell the story.

It is an amazing story and not without controversy, since Weiss said that he and his fellow officers turned a few of those they caught—specifically, members of the SS's notorious Death's Head branch—over to the death camp survivors who were housed in huge displaced person camps after the war. There was no ambiguity about what would happen—the Nazis would be killed. Weiss told the *Post* that he never regretted the fate of those SS fugitives. "The jails were full," he said. "They were going to slip through the cracks."

But it is the story of finding Hitler's will that is the most amazing of all, and on Wednesday, I couldn't help asking Weiss to repeat it. He and a colleague had located Martin Bormann's adjutant, Wilhelm Zander, who told them he had been dispatched from Hitler's infamous bunker with important papers given him by Hitler just before the end. "I suppose you want the documents," Zander told Weiss.

With that, Zander directed Weiss and his colleague to a dry well behind an isolated farmhouse, from which was retrieved a briefcase containing a plain manila envelope.

Weiss tore it open. It was in his native German, and

he recognized instantly that he was looking at Hitler's will, which indicated the tyrant was taking his own life rather than become a prisoner on parade.

I told Weiss I was getting goose bumps just listening to the story. What must have it been like, 60 years ago, to realize what he held in his hands?

"I was flabbergasted," he said.

───────────

Friday, July 29, 2005

Now 75 Square Miles of Unreality

Dave Davis, geographic information system coordinator for the city of Madison's Engineering Department, wants you to know that your city is composed of 75.77 square miles.

It is up to the rest of us to decide whether that 75.77 square miles is "surrounded by reality."

Davis ran some numbers Wednesday to come up with the figure, which is subject to change, what with annexations and the give and take that has always transpired between cities and towns.

It's also subject to interpretation among the officials whose job it is to tabulate it. Davis said that Engineering's figure is routinely a bit lower than the square mileage total calculated by the Planning and Development Department.

Because Engineering is concerned with the land area for which it maintains city services, Davis omits Monona Bay and Lake Wingra from his total.

Planning and Development, he said, does not omit those bodies of water and consequently has a slightly higher figure.

Surrounded by Reality

Bill Lanier, geographic information specialist with Planning and Development, said Thursday that his department does include Lake Wingra in its total, but not Monona Bay. "Lake Wingra was annexed in," Lanier said. "Monona Bay was not."

He also mentioned that the Arboretum was annexed into the city two summers ago, so the current figure is higher than the 68.78 square miles Lanier quoted to me back in December 1999. As we spoke this week, Lanier began pushing some buttons to see if he could get me a current Planning and Development figure on the square mileage of Madison.

Although the methodologies of both Engineering and Planning and Development make sense, it would be nice if we could settle on one number, or at least one methodology, since the borders are always going to be subject to tweaking.

The reason one number is important is that it makes it a little easier to handle when a Republican legislator or anyone else looking for a quick putdown of the city refers to us as so many square miles "surrounded by reality."

It's still annoying, but it's more annoying when everyone gets the number wrong.

I first tried to address this gravely important issue six years ago. I had received a friendly press release that noted in an aside that surely I realized Madison was "15 square miles surrounded by reality."

I snapped. I knew that former governor Lee Dreyfus had originally hung the label on us. A top Dreyfus aide, Bill Kraus, told me he remembered Dreyfus on the campaign stump referring to Madison as "30 square miles surrounded by reality."

Dreyfus left town after one term and left the rest of us with his "reality" label. With just a moment's research I found all kinds of people who had seized on it, either quoting Dreyfus's incorrect number or getting it wrong on their own.

For example, in a 1995 guest column in the *Cap Times,* County Exec Rick Phelps wrote, "When Gov. Dreyfus characterized Madison as 78 square miles surrounded by reality." Or travel consultant Bill Geist in 1991: "Madison really is 50 square miles surrounded by reality." Radio personality John "Sly" Sylvester in 1995: "Madison is 25 square miles surrounded by reality." The late maverick Gene Parks in 1998: "Madison is 24 square miles surrounded by reality."

As a public service, in 1999, I called Lanier in Planning and Development, and he gave me the 68.78 square miles figure. I publicized it as best I could, but people still got it wrong.

In March of 2004, Mike Kessler wrote a letter to the *State Journal* noting that Madison is "60 square miles surrounded by reality." Just this past May, a columnist for that paper, whom I will identify only as Susan Lampert Smith, was writing about Madison as a girl's first name and noted, "She'll live in her own world: 16 square miles surrounded by reality."

Now on Thursday Lanier at Planning and Development was running his numbers and eventually came up with a figure: According to his department, Madison is 76.23 square miles.

That's opposed to the Engineering Department's 75.77 square miles.

Maybe, for simplicity's sake, we can settle on a round figure of 75 square miles.

Or maybe we will just have to live in a constant state of confusion, since the number is subject to change anyway, and to be confused in Madison is to be at one with the city's overall karma.

For instance, on Thursday, I was chatting with Lanier when he noted, "I've always wondered about John Nolen Drive."

Surrounded by Reality

He was referring to the much-traveled road into downtown that separates Monona Bay from the rest of the lake.

"What do you mean?"

Well, Lanier said, as far as he could tell it had never been annexed into the city of Madison.

"Is it in the town?"

"I'm not sure," he said. "Maybe it's in the lake."

About the Author

Doug Moe, a lifelong Madisonian, has written a daily newspaper column about the city for *The Capital Times* since 1997. He has also been editor of *Madison Magazine* and written several books, including *The World of Mike Royko*, a *Chicago Tribune* Choice Selection of the Year, and, most recently, *Lords of the Ring: The Triumph and Tragedy of College Boxing's Greatest Team*, which is on the *Chronicle of Higher Education's* list of the best college sports books of all time. He has won journalism awards from the State Bar of Wisconsin and the Wisconsin Newspaper Association. In 2005 he was voted best columnist in two readers polls, one conducted by *Madison Magazine* and the other by the *Wisconsin State Journal* and *The Capital Times*.